Plant Containers
You Can Make

By the Editors of Sunset Books and Sunset Magazine

Lane Publishing Co. · Menlo Park, California

A different kind of garden book....

The pages that follow contain no long Latin plant names—in fact, the amount of plant information is almost nil. Instead, this book turns to the unsung hero of the gardening world, the plant container.

In researching this book, the editors of *Sunset* combed a number of craft fields to come up with an array of designs for attractive tubs, pots, and boxes. Because wooden containers continue to be immensely popular, you will find a number of them in this book; however, if woodworking is not your thing, you might want to try one of the examples that utilize some other technique. Macramé, perhaps (pages 76-77). Or leatherwork (pages 78-79). Or metal sculpture (pages 68-69).

If making a container from scratch doesn't appeal to you, consider the suggestions for giving store bought pots a facelift. You will find ideas for putting kitchen ware, antiques, and miscellaneous building materials to use as plant containers. A separate section focuses on designs for planters that are built right into a house.

There are ideas here for everyone, newcomers to gardening as well as seasoned green thumbers. Some of the pots work best for indoor plants; some will go indoors or out. All were selected with an eye to combining simplicity with originality.

We would like to give special thanks to the following people for their thoughtful contribution and participation in bringing this book together: Myrtle Anderson, Carol Goforth, Neil Heneweer, Lynne Morrall, Bill Penfield, Roy Rydell, and Don Spradlin.

Edited by Robyn E. Shotwell

Design and Artwork: Joe Seney

Cover: Redwood cubes (see *Ying Yang Cube,* pages 46-47), designed by John August; glazed clay pot (see *New Glazes for New Faces,* pages 42-43). Photographed by Ells Marugg.

Executive Editor, Sunset Books: David E. Clark

First Printing February 1976

Table of Contents

Brilliant colors flow *around undulating sides of a macramé decorative sleeve. (See pages 76-77 for instructions.) Design: Nilda Duffek.*

Rose hue *of copper planter casts warm light in any setting. Graceful false spiraea spills over irregular pipe ends of container. (See pages 68-69 for instructions.) Design: Hal Pastorius.*

Sheep liver can, *recycled as practical plant container, holds windowside greenery in a Yorkshire home in England.*

Container Know-how in a Nutshell

A plant's home can be its castle if you take the time and care to provide a decorative, tasteful container.

Let your imagination go. Have you ever thought of a nutshell as a container? Well, it is one. And so are countless other objects—an old wine barrel, a coconut shell, a discarded coffee can, a piece of driftwood. "Creative containery" is at your finger tips, whether your skills are as basic as cutting a piece of leather or pasting a piece of paper, or as advanced as sawing a mitered edge or soldering copper pipes.

Choosing a container

Careful thought is necessary to assure a happy marriage between a plant and its container. Even in the plant container world, not all marriages are a result of love at first sight. Sometimes you have to experiment by switching plants from one container to another until you find the perfect match.

Waterproof construction: Make containers from waterproof materials. If this is not feasible, waterproof the container with several coats of polyurethane varnish. Some materials (cloth, reeds) need extra waterproofing—using plastic or foil on the inside of the container will give protection from moisture.

Compatibility of room, container, and plant: Look at the colors, light, textures, mood of the room in which the plant will be. Let these factors guide your choice of a container that complements the plant and blends with its surroundings.

Color, texture, and—more importantly—size are crucial to deciding how a plant can harmonize with

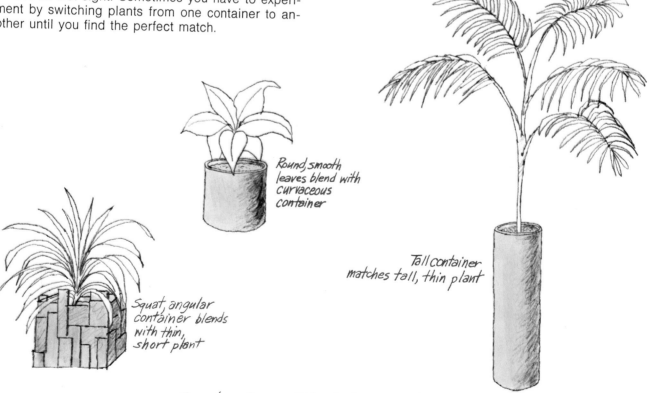

Round, smooth leaves blend with curvaceous container

Squat, angular container blends with thin, short plant

Tall container matches tall, thin plant

Examples of compatible plants and containers

its container. An awareness of size reveals that tall, lanky plants appear balanced in tall containers; short, shrublike plants are at their best in short, decorative containers.

See drawings, page 4, for suggestions on choosing plants and containers that complement each other.

Drainage: Poor drainage is a plant's most dangerous and, unfortunately, most common enemy. For successful container gardening, all containers should have adequate drainage.

Containers fall into three categories:

• Containers with drainage holes: These should be set on trays or saucers to catch excess water that drains through the pot after watering.

• Containers without drainage holes that serve as decorative holders for purchased clay or plastic pots: Use a layer of gravel or pot shards between the pot and the outer container to allow drainage.

• Containers without drainage, planted directly inside: Layering of soil and gravel is essential to the plant's survival in these containers. Layering prevents the collection of moisture that would eventually cause root rot. Soil and gravel can be layered in this way:

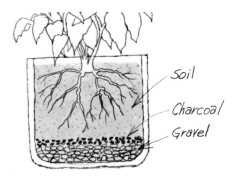

Soil
Charcoal
Gravel

Caring for plants in containers

Without going into great detail about plant care, here are some of the basic guidelines for keeping your plants alive and well in containers. Consult the Sunset book *Gardening in Containers* for more information on each point.

• Water regularly according to the needs of each plant. All plants don't require the same amount of water at the same time intervals. Each plant has its own needs based on the amount and type of soil in the container, the plant's root structure, the sunlight and ventilation it receives, and the kind of plant it is.

To find out when to water, test the soil with your finger. If the soil is dry an inch below the surface, it's time to water. Other ways to find out if the plant needs water: see if the foliage is drooping or drying out; tap the pot—if it has a light, hollow sound, it is time to water. Plants without adequate drainage need water less often and in smaller quantities than those with good drainage.

There are several methods of watering. Soak the potted plant in a sink or tub full of water and then let the pot drain completely. Or use a watering can or watering funnel.

• Fertilize plants regularly according to the requirements of the plant species, the time of year, and the size of container.

Fertilizers come in different forms. Each has its own special instructions which should be carefully followed. Be consistent with your feeding schedule.

• Pinching and pruning plants increases growth and improves appearance. Pruning pertains not only to the top foliage but also to the roots.

Root pruning

• Repot plants when they become too large for their containers. Follow the steps below for repotting and for transplanting plants from nursery containers to your own handcrafted containers.

Transplanting technique

1. Remove plant from container

2. Set plant on layer of soil. Drainage hole is covered with pot shards

3. Add soil around edges

4. Tap container on a hard surface to settle soil around plant

• Keep the leaves clean by washing them with plain water and a soft cloth.

• Be aware of your plant's health. Study plant disease descriptions and become familiar with the causes and cures of the ills that befall plants. Read instructions carefully before using plant sprays and solutions.

Plant Stands and Pot Holders

Hanging by lips, *pots hold marigold, sweet broom, and azalea. Design: Tim Campbell.*

Plant stands and pot holders can bless your plants with greater mobility, accessibility, and visibility.

Even the most pedestrian planter gains pizzazz if it's raised off the ground. An example is the common clay pot—a good candidate for getting a lift. Clay pots blend especially well with wooden pot holders because of the rough, natural essence of the two materials.

One of the simplest ways to bring plants closer to eye level is to place a pot on a pedestal; another is to put a planter box on stilts. A possible disadvan- tage, though, is that these plant stands become part of the containers and diminish their mobility. Use these methods if mobility is not a consideration.

For the ultimate in container mobility, use plant stands that have their own wheels. Large outdoor containers are obvious candidates for the use of wheels. When your landscape design changes—re- quiring a new arrangement of your largest containers —your best defense against a sprained back or wrenched muscle is a plant stand on casters or rubber wheels.

Redwood Pot Bench

The humble clay pot is usually plopped down on an outdoor deck or placed in a leftover saucer on a window sill. There—in splendid isolation—it loses the effect it might have if it were grouped with other pots and effectively displayed.

The redwood plant bench is one solution that performs two functions: it holds and displays clay-potted plants, lifting them above the ground and closer to eye level. It also serves as a piece of furniture with decorative value—to break up large, monotonous deck spaces or inside living spaces.

The bench is made of redwood so that it will last if used outdoors. Notches act as fasteners for the top and bottom braces, making the unit sturdy and tight enough to bear the weight of the filled pots. Left unglued, the entire plant bench can be dis- assembled for moving. Or if perma- nence and additional stability are your goals, glue and nail all the joints.

Materials and tools

Clear, all-heart redwood as follows:
Four 18-inch 2 by 4s
Four 14-inch 2 by 2s
Two 40-inch 2 by 6s
One 40-inch 2 by 4
Table or radial-arm saw
Waterproof glue
8-penny galvanized nails/hammer
Tape measure
Pencil/compass
Sandpaper/stain (optional)
Saber saw
Note: If you don't have a table or radial-arm saw to cut the notches, use nails to fasten the joints.

How to make

1. Select three 8-inch clay pots. The pot measurement refers to the diameter of the pot below its lip. Double check this measurement when buying the pot. (These direc- tions may be adapted for use with pots of other sizes.)

2. With a table saw, cut a dado groove 2 inches from each end of the 4 legs. The dadoes should be cut to receive the 2 by 2-inch cross supports (fig. 1). Attach the cross supports to the legs at the points where the cross supports fit into the dadoes. Make sure the cross supports are flush with the outside edge.

3. To make the top section, lay the 2 by 6s side by side. Measuring down the center where the 2 boards meet, make a mark 4 inches in from each end to show where the outside edge of each circle begins. From each mark, measure in 4 more inches for the center of each outside circle, and draw the 8-inch circles, using the compass. Leave 4 inches between each outside circle and the 8-inch circle in the center.

4. After drawing all 3 circum- ferences, cut out the circles with a saber saw.

5. Dado the bottom of the 2 by 6s, measuring 2 inches from each end. With a table saw, cut a dado to receive the 2 by 2-inch cross sup- ports (fig. 2). The dadoes should be 1½ inches wide and ½ inch deep.

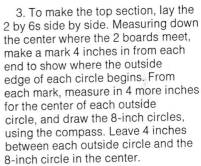

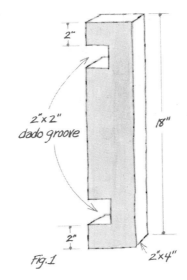

Fig. 1

2" x 2" dado groove

18"

2" x 4"

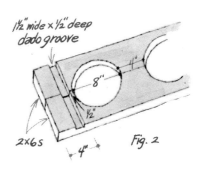

1½" wide x ½" deep dado groove

8"

2×6s

4"

Fig. 2

6. Notch the bottom brace (40- inch 2 by 4) in the same way.

7. Assemble the bench, leaving joints loose or gluing and nailing them. Add flower pots.

Containers on the Move

Moving large, heavy containers from one location to another could require superhuman strength. But there are alternatives to brute force—given a set of wheels or rollers, containers glide easily from one place to another.

Here are three ways to use rollers to give large plants greater mobility:

The rolling pedestal planter. This tall planter is simple to build and raises your plant even closer to eye level. You can leave the wood natural or paint it to blend with a room's color scheme. Almost any kind of indoor plant will thrive in the top in a clay pot with a saucer. All the wood parts are made of ½-inch plywood (fig. 1).

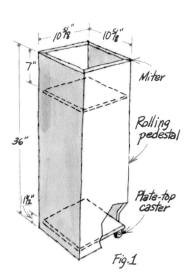

10⅝" 10⅝"
7"
Miter
Rolling pedestal
36"
1½"
Plate-top caster
Fig. 1

Pedestals and Stilts

Raising a plant off the ground has several advantages. One is to free floor space—helpful where space is at a premium. Another is that raised plants become a decorative element, working better with the overall room design. Finally, you can better appreciate both the plant and the container when they're at eye level.

One way to give your plants a lift is to use wood blocks. Four large redwood blocks combine to make a simple, contemporary-looking plant stand.

Materials and tools

4 blocks of clear redwood 4 by 4s
(The length depends on desired height of plant stands. Width can also vary, depending on the size of containers.)
One 6-inch redwood square, 2 inches thick, for the base
Two ½ by 2¼-inch lath spacers
Sandpaper
9 and 3-penny nails/hammer
Handsaw

How to make

1. With a saw, cut the 4 by 4 into desired lengths to get 4 equal blocks. Sand all surfaces.
2. Use two ½ by 2¼-inch spacers to connect pairs of blocks diagonally. Nail them near the middle and bottom (fig. 1).

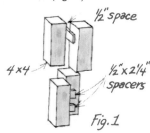

½" space
4×4
½" × 2¼" spacers
Fig. 1

3. Slip the pairs together. Center and nail on the square base (fig. 2).

Plant container
Fig. 2
2"×6"×6" base

Stilts offer another way to elevate plants. For a pleasing use of stilts, set a collection of small boxes at different heights. A long, narrow container is the base, and dowel legs of varying lengths support the boxes. You can construct as many containers in as many sizes as you want. The effect is a layered jungle of greenery. Grouped this way, the plants give different impressions from every angle.

The entire planter is easily moved by two people—just lift the box by the handles on either end.

Materials and tools

Clear, all-heart redwood as follows:
8 feet of 1 by 8
36 inches of 1 by 12
42 inches of 1 by 2
Waterproof glue
6-penny nails/hammer
Clear polyurethane varnish/brush
Pencil/handsaw
Wood rasp/clamps
Drill/¼-inch bit

Materials for small containers

Wood scraps or assorted sizes of wood (5/16 to ⅜-inch thickness)
Nails: at least twice as long as your wood is thick
Doweling: ¼-inch diameter (enough for 2 to 4 legs for each container; varying heights)

How to make

1. With a handsaw, cut the 1 by 8-inch redwood into two 1-foot lengths and two 3-foot lengths.
2. Cut out a 3 by 4-inch piece from each end of the 3-foot lengths

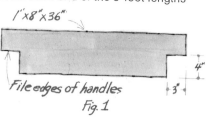

1"×8"×36"
4"
File edges of handles
3"
Fig. 1

The rolling plant stage. This is the most practical way to move your plants around. If you're an experienced container gardener, you know that raising pots and tubs a few inches off the ground on a platform enhances both the plants and the containers. Build the platform with several 1 by 6s supported by two 1 by 4s. Add a caster at each corner and you have a true movable feast of greenery (fig. 2).

Fig. 2

The circular plant base. You can make even the most ponderous plant mobile by placing the container on a circular base mounted on four casters. Construct the base the same size as the base of the container, using 1-inch exterior plywood. Cut out a circle in its center to hold an aluminum pie pan for catching

Sawed out center *holds aluminum pan. Design: Col. and Mrs. T. Harris.*

water. Attach four casters to the bottom of the base, setting them in far enough from the edge to conceal them. Nail two reinforcing boards of 1-inch lumber across the bottom between the wheels.

To empty the water pan, you must lift the plant, but this is rarely necessary if you water judiciously.

Ball-bearing casters, *screwed to base, are set in so they don't touch skirt.*

---

to form the handles. File edges to make handles easier to hold (fig. 1).

3. Trim the 36-inch 1 by 12 to 28 inches for the bottom piece.

4. Cut the 42-inch 1 by 2 into three 12¾-inch lengths for reinforcing strips.

5. Glue and nail the two 1-foot pieces to the bottom board (fig. 2).

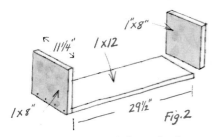

11¼"   1 x 12   1"x8"

1"x8"   29½"   Fig. 2

6. Glue, nail, and clamp the two 3-foot sides to the bottom and ends of the container. Nail the 1 by 2 strips across top of box (fig. 3).

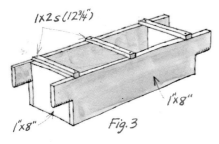

1x2s (12¾")

1"x8"   1"x8"   Fig. 3

7. With a drill and a ¼-inch bit, drill several holes in the base for drainage.

8. Construct the small containers in various sizes, using butt joints

and following the diagram below. Fasten with glue and 3 nails on each corner (fig. 4).

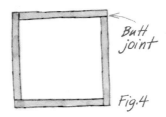

Butt joint

Fig. 4

9. Make a second, smaller base for each container. Drill 1 or 2 holes in the base to receive the dowels. Glue the second base to the first base of each container (fig. 5).

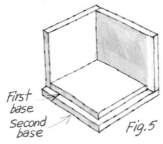

First base
Second base   Fig. 5

10. From doweling, cut 2 or 4 legs for each box. Cut varying lengths, but 8 inches is minimum because dowels must rest on the bottom of the large box. Glue the dowels in small container bases (fig. 6).

11. Cover the entire container—the large box, dowels, and small boxes—with several coats of clear polyurethane varnish. Let dry.

12. Spread a layer of gravel on the bottom of the large box. Arrange

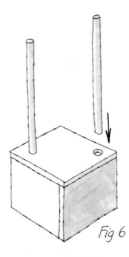

Fig 6

the smaller boxes in the large one, adding soil to hold legs in place. Firm the soil around the base of each dowel and continue adding soil to within an inch of the top of the large box.

13. Fill the small containers with potting soil and plant. You can also plant the large box with a low ground cover like baby tears.

Layered jungle *of greenery is effect of multilevel planter. Design: David Totel.*

Plywood Pot Stand

This plant stand is in a class by itself—the corners are rounded and the edges are coated with clear varnish, making the most of the natural wood grain. Easily put together, the plant stand is constructed of plywood or particle board. (If particle board is used, the edges should be painted with a solid color.)

Set almost any type of container—including a plain clay pot—on this stand. If you use a container with drainage, place a saucer on the stand underneath the pot. This design holds an 8-inch pot with a saucer, but you can vary the dimensions to suit pots of any size.

Materials and tools

30 by 24-inch piece of ¾-inch
   A/A birch plywood
Electric or hand drill/½-inch,
   3/32-inch, and 1½-inch
   countersinking bits
1½-inch #8 screws/screwdriver
Wood rasp
Waterproof glue
Handsaw or saber saw
Polyurethane varnish/brush
Rubber feet
Pencil
Wood filler/putty knife
Sandpaper (80 and 120 grit)
Straightedge/clamp

(Continued in next column)

4 inches pine or fir 2 by 2
¾-inch masking tape

How to make

1. Lay out 4 vertical pieces on a sheet of 24 by 30-inch plywood as shown below (fig. 1).

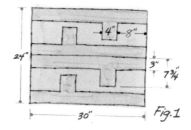

Fig. 1

2. With a drill and a ½-inch bit, drill a hole on all inside corners, making sure that the circumference of each hole aligns with the vertical and horizontal edges (fig. 2).

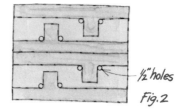

½" holes

Fig. 2

3. Cut out all the pieces, using a handsaw. You may want to clamp a straightedge (piece of wood, aluminum, etc.) on the cutting lines to ensure straight cuts if you use a saber saw (fig. 3).

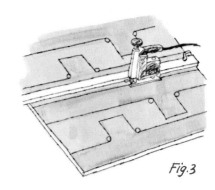

Fig. 3

4. With a wood rasp, round all corners (fig. 4).

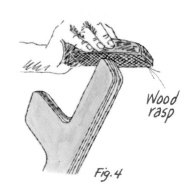

Wood rasp

Fig. 4

Hanging Pot Holder

A square frame of redwood is a cozy nest for clay pots. The pot holder is simple to make, requiring no hardware or glue to assemble. The pots are easily removed for watering, and the entire holder is collapsible.

Plant your pots with herbs and hang in a kitchen window. Discover how convenient it is to snip off a few herbs for seasoning. You can also use this pot holder outdoors. If you do so, seal the wood with a wood sealer.

Materials and tools

7 feet of clear redwood 1 by 2
(Continued in next column)

Four 4-inch clay pots
¼-inch manila rope (length
   depends on how high you want
   your pots to hang)
Table saw or handsaw
Drill/⅜-inch bit
Scissors

How to make

1. Cut the redwood 1 by 2 into five 15-inch lengths.
2. Notch 2 of these to use as side supports. With a table saw or handsaw, cut notches about 3/16 inch deep and wide enough to accept a 1 by 2; notches should be spaced about 4¼ inches apart to accommodate 4-inch pots (fig. 1). Each of the 2 side supports will have 3 notches.

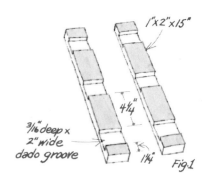

1"x2"x15"

4¼"

3/16" deep x 2" wide dado groove

1¼"

Fig. 1

3. Letting the 1 by 2s project about 1 inch at the corners, fit the upper 3 pieces into 2 lower notched pieces. Drill a ⅜-inch hole through corner overlaps.

5. Sand all edges and faces, first rubbing gently with the 80 grit and then with the 120 grit sandpaper.

6. If plywood has voids on the cut edges, fill them with wood filler in a color that blends with the wood.

7. With a drill and 3/32-inch bit, drill 2 pilot holes in each of the 4 pieces. Use the countersinking bit and redrill the holes (fig. 5).

8. Attach the 4-inch 2 by 2 to 1 leg by first gluing and then screwing the 2 pieces together. Be sure to countersink the screws. Glue and screw the remaining pieces to the 2 by 2.

9. Smooth over the screws, using wood filler. When the filler dries, sand over and around the screws.

10. Coat the edges with a clear polyurethane varnish. When dry, mask the edges with masking tape and then coat the faces with an opaque polyurethane varnish.

11. Attach rubber feet to the bottoms of the 4 legs if the plant stand is to be used on a hard-surfaced floor.

Leafy piggyback *softens angles of plant stand. Design: Donald William MacDonald.*

4. Cut 2 equal lengths of ¼-inch manila rope for hanging the holder. Fit the boards into the notches. Thread each end of the rope through the holes and tie knots underneath the supports (fig. 2).

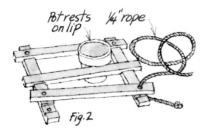

5. Hang the pot holder from the ceiling using a sturdy screw hook or toggle hook.

Quartet of pots *clusters in notched redwood holder. Design: Skip Johnson.*

Pots on Posts

Why let structural posts look like barren tree trunks? Add a touch of greenery to them, breaking up their stark surfaces and creating a decorative element for a covered patio. Shelves, clips, or pot holders are all you need to transform run-of-the-mill posts into good-looking plant stands.

Gardening on a post works particularly well for plants that cascade or are more effective at eye level: fuchsias, succulents, staghorn ferns. You can try almost anything, but trailing plants that cover the containers usually look best.

It's a bit tricky to water a collection of pots attached to a post. If you're a good judge of how much a pot will hold without dripping, then you can water the plants in place, giving them small amounts of water daily rather than an occasional dousing.

For another approach to dripless in-place watering, you may want to attach circular holders to a post; the holders will serve as saucers for the pots. Or hang a saucer from a pot itself, using chains attached to the lip of the pot.

If you prefer, you can remove all the plants once a week and give them a good soaking in the bathtub or kitchen sink. Allow them to drain well before you replace them.

Post holds herbs in clay pots that slip into cutouts in round redwood platform. To build, clamp four 1 by 12 by 24-inch boards in two layers, grains crossing. Use jigsaw or saber saw to cut wood into 24-inch circle, make circular cutouts for 6-inch pots and square hole for post. Unclamp, reassemble around base of post, and nail two layers together. Raise to desired height; support with wood blocks nailed to post.

Cluster of boxes clings to 6 by 6-inch post. Four boxes of rugged redwood hold Sprenger asparagus. Each box is 6 by 8 by 10 inches. Decorative blocks are nailed to bottoms of boxes. Blocks consist of a 1 by 4, a 4 by 4, and a 2 by 2 of redwood. Post plants break up monotony of vertical posts, make use of scrap wood. Decorative boxes are alternatives for hanging planters for outdoor decks and patios.

Crisscrossed pairs of redwood strips support four 6-inch clay pots. Redwood supports are ½ by 1 by 21 inches. Post that serves as center for supports is 6 by 6 redwood. Quarter-inch dowels span ends of redwood supports to secure pots. Sedum and string of pearls fill these pots; herbs are even more effective.

Bonsai shelves are platforms of varied sizes clustered around a single post. Each has ½ by 2-inch slats nailed to pairs of 1 by 2s. Platforms are positioned to suit heights of various bonsai plants. Containers remove easily for watering and plant maintenance.

Clip-on pot holders, inexpensive at garden supply stores, hold pots up to 7 inches wide. Use screws or galvanized nails to fasten clips. Attach clips to posts after pots have been planted, considering outline of both plant and pot as you plan arrangement. Because of metal projection that fits under pot's lip, holders can support surprisingly heavy loads. Outdoors or in, clips are quick and easy means for plant arrangement.

Hanging Containers

Transparent hanging container *shows off grape ivy and layers of gravel and soil. Design: Hawley Adams, Transpose Co.*

Acrylic Container

The beauty of an acrylic container lies in its transparency. The combined effects of soil, plants, and light shine through the crystal-like material. Light glances off the cut edges of the geometric shape, creating an illusion of milky white lines.

Because this planter has no drainage holes, you'll need to include a layer of charcoal, sand, gravel, or vermiculite when you plant your greenery. You may prefer to drill drainage holes in the bottom with a ¼-inch drill bit followed by a cone-shaped bit to enlarge the ¼-inch holes.

If the container develops leaks, use a plastic sealant to caulk all the seams.

Materials and tools

13½ by 16½-inch sheet of acrylic plastic, 3/16 inch thick
Solvent cement applicator (a small bottle with a long needle)
1 bottle of solvent cement, #3 or #4
2 pieces of 25 weight fishing line, each 40 inches long
Wooden bead
Curtain ring
Brick/paper toweling
Scribing tool
Electric or hand drill/⅛-inch bit
Propane torch/matches
Fine grade sandpaper
Framing square
Felt-tipped pen/crayon
Commercial acrylic plastic cleaner
Soft rag

Why hang on to conventional ways of displaying plants? It's high time to consider hanging plants in containers. Plants suspended from rafters, beams, and ceilings break up spaces, add variety to your arrangement of plants, and provide color in an unexpected place.

Some containers—like those in this chapter—are designed especially for hanging. But a little ingenuity, an attractive hanger, and a sturdy fastener can transform almost any container into the start of a colorful hanging garden.

The "where to hang it" question deserves advance thought. Because filled plant containers are heavy, you'll need a strong support such as a beam or a sturdy tree branch. If it's going in an area where people walk, the container must hang high enough so that heads won't bump against it. Consider sun, wind, and shade conditions just as you would for more conventional planting.

What about dripping water? Attached saucers are insurance against having water streaming over indoor and outdoor flooring and furniture.

How to make

1. Leave the protective masking paper on the sheet of acrylic to protect the plastic from scratches during construction of the planter. With a felt-tipped pen, draw the planter pieces on the protective paper, using the measurements below. Mark each piece with the correct letter.

2. With the scribing tool in one hand, hold the plastic firmly with the other hand. Carefully, but firmly, draw the blade over the lines repeatedly until the cuts are made (fig. 1).

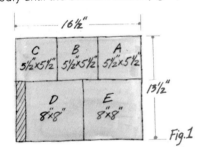

Fig. 1

3. Take the masking paper off the 3 inside pieces (A, B, C) and, with the crayon, lightly mark each piece again with its identifying letter.

4. Wrap the brick in paper toweling and place it on its side on a table to create a 90° angle. Position piece A flat on the table with 1 edge abutting the brick. Stand piece B against the brick, perpendicular to A, aligning the 5½-inch sides for a precise fit (fig. 2).

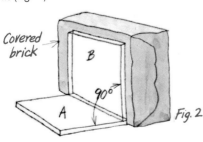

Covered brick

Fig. 2

5. Holding B in place, slowly draw the needle of the glue applicator along the seam. The glue will give the seam a watery color. Let the glue dry for 15 minutes.

6. Turn the joined pieces around so that the opposite edge of A is now against the brick. Place piece C against the brick parallel to B, making sure that the 5½-inch side fits precisely. Holding piece C in place, glue as you did in step 5. Let the glue dry for 15 minutes. The U-shaped portion of the planter is complete.

7. Remove the protective paper from pieces D and E. Fit D into the right angle of the framing square. Place the ABC unit on the surface of D so that both corners of 1 U-shaped side of ABC reach 2 edges of D about 4 inches from the lower point of the square. The U-shaped form makes a triangle with the bottom corner of piece D (fig. 3).

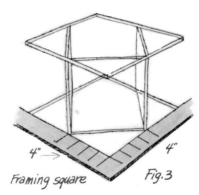

Framing square   Fig. 3

8. Begin gluing the seams, making sure the glue is applied evenly. After gluing, gently place the covered brick on the top to ensure a tight seal. Let the glue dry for several hours.

9. Place piece E in the same position in the framing square. Turn the planter over and follow the same procedure as in steps 7 and 8. Wait 24 hours before flaming the edges.

10. Light a propane torch and turn it to a low flame. Place the planter on its side so that it overhangs the edge of the table by about 1 inch. With the torch, slowly run the flame along the edges of the planter. Just the tip of the blue flame should touch the plastic. Otherwise, the plastic may start to burn. If the plastic starts to burn, you are either going too slowly or holding the torch too close. Just blow out the flame on the plastic and proceed.

11. If the edges still show the cutting marks, sand with a fine grade sandpaper and reflame.

12. With a ⅛-inch drill bit, drill 2 small holes in piece B and 2 in A at the top corners (fig. 4).

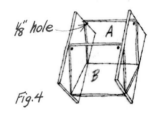

⅛" hole

Fig. 4

13. Starting from the outside in, thread each side with a 40-inch piece of fishing line. Draw the lines together at the top and string the 4 pieces of line through a bead. Tie the 4 pieces at the top onto a curtain ring, using a simple knot (fig. 5).

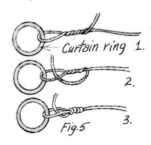

Curtain ring 1.

2.

Fig. 5 3.

14. Clean your completed container with a commercial acrylic cleaner. Plant and hang.

Slings, Hooks, and Cradles

Hang pots with a variety of materials: inexpensive leather thongs blend with clay pots; metal hooks interlock to hold pots; macramé cord and hemp make hangers for suspending gourds and ceramic pots of all sizes.

Enhance free-flowing plants with a macramé sling. If you have a creative bent and flexible hands for knot tying, try making your own sling.

Pot hanger hides in trellis, suspended from 1 by 2s joined by dowels at top and bottom.

Dog leash lock spring, hook, built-in swivel, and its chain are inexpensive components for hanger.

Four for hanging (clockwise from top): plastic pot with clip-on saucer, fern pot with lip-type wire hanger, clay hanging pot, oriental bowl in macramé sling.

Fishing tackle swivel hangs between two hooks, lets you rotate plant for light on all sides.

Bent nail and metal plumber's tape hang on wire hook. Hook will hold hanging planters.

Cotton cable cord, brass ring, four ceramic dangles or large-holed beads are basic ingredients for macramé hanger. Entire project uses square knots.

Hanging Baskets without Soil

Start with a mélange of moss, soil, wire, and plants and transform it all into growing masses of greenery or bright cascades of flowers. Suspended from beams and ceilings or used as decorative accents on walls or fences, hanging wire baskets bring a fresh touch and a splash of color.

Garden suppliers sell manufactured wire forms that will give you the basic shapes. Or you can create more exotic forms using chicken wire. Either way, the basic idea is to create a container from a wire form lined with moss.

The care and feeding of the finished container is uncomplicated: water daily or every other day, depending on the weather; fertilize every 2 weeks. To check whether or not a basket needs water, feel the bottom. If it's oozing with moisture, don't water. When a basket does need a drink, water by filling the top several times until water gushes out the bottom.

Materials and tools

Manufactured wire form or chicken wire for homemade form
Sphagnum moss (quantity depends on size of form)
Shears
Vitamin B1
Potting soil
Fertilizer
Small plants
Tub/water

How to make

1. Place the sphagnum moss in a tub filled with water and soak the moss until it becomes spongy and pliable.
2. Pack the bottom of the wire form until the moss is 1 to 1½ inches thick. Make sure the moss is packed halfway through the wire (fig. 1).

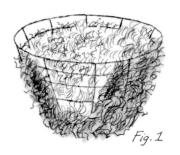

Fig. 1

3. Carefully work up the sides of the form. When you reach the top of the form, make a well-packed, firm shoulder. Begin working the moss into the vertical posts and then make a complete ring using the top 2 wires. This is an essential step: if the shoulder is weak it will soon blow or wash away, causing water and soil to spill out of the container (fig. 2).

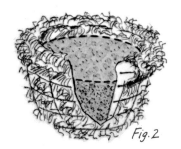

Fig. 2

4. With your fingers, press the entire moss-laden form one more time and let dry for 24 hours.
5. Trim all the excess moss from the form with shears until you have a clean, compact shape. Save the trimmings for use on future containers.
6. You are now ready to plant the container, using small plants with compact root balls. Wet the entire container thoroughly. Starting from the bottom and working quickly up the sides, cut plugs out of the moss with shears, bending the wire where necessary to create small openings for the root balls. Work the plant into the openings, making sure the roots reach the interior cavity. Press more bits of moss in under the wire around the plants. Avoid planting near the shoulder and at the very bottom of the container. Make sure the plants are firmly embedded into the form.
7. Fill the container with potting soil, tamping it down as you fill. Cover all the roots that protrude into the interior. Put more plants directly into the soil at the top.
8. Place in a shady location. Fertilize the plants with Vitamin B1 and water the entire basket thoroughly. After a few days' rest in shade, the basket can be moved to a sunnier spot, depending on the kinds of plants you've used.

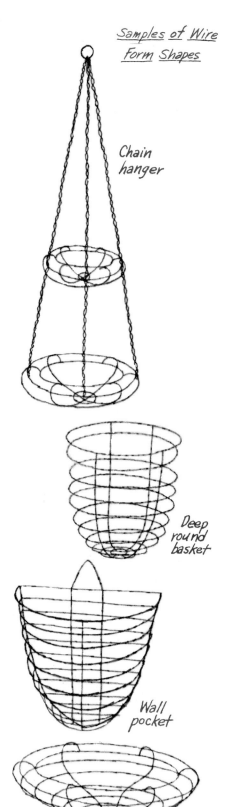

Samples of Wire Form Shapes

Chain hanger

Deep round basket

Wall pocket

Sombrero

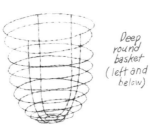

Deep round basket (left and below)

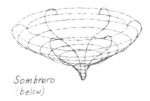

Sombrero (below)

Spherical wire form *provides shape for tightly packed hanging basket of whites, greens. Bedding begonias are good planting materials for hardy outdoor hanging baskets.*

Delicate blooms and greenery *include a few miniature roses and clumps of sweet alyssum, lobelia, and ivy geranium.*

Dish-shaped wire form *holds English ivy, Algerian ivy, grape ivy, Sprenger asparagus, busy Lizzie, and Japanese aralia.*

Dangling Diamond for Ferns

Distinctive diamond-shaped *wooden hanging planter is outdoor home for trailing ferns. Design: John Sheard.*

This distinctive, diamond-shaped hanging wooden planter is a geometric nest for Sprenger asparagus, ivy, ivy geraniums, hanging succulents, or other trailing plants. It is best used outdoors; water tends to drip after a generous watering. Use a chain and eyebolt for hanging the planter from a sturdy support. Planting space at the soil line is about 6 by 16 inches. If you like, you can drill small holes near the bottom for drainage.

Materials and tools

21 feet of 2 by 2-inch redwood
3 feet of 1 by 12-inch redwood
Table saw or handsaw and
   miter box
10-penny galvanized nails/hammer
Clear polyurethane varnish/brush
Chain/Eyebolt

Pockets for Walls

Fan-shaped pockets tastefully break the monotony of blank wall spaces. Wall planters like this one can hold dried arrangements, cut flowers, or small house plants.

You don't need sophisticated equipment or a knowledge of ceramic techniques. You can even do without a kiln by arranging to have your planter fired by a ceramics dealer. Be sure to ask what glazes to use with the type of clay you buy.

Materials and tools

4 pounds clay containing either
   sand or grog
Table knife
Paper towels
Size #3 knitting needle
Copper penny
Paper/pencil
Scissors
Cloth-covered cutting board
Rolling pin or 2-inch doweling
2 strips of ¼-inch-thick wood

How to make

1. Use a pencil, paper, and scissors to make a kite-shaped pattern about 8 inches high and 8 inches wide. The exact dimensions aren't crucial, for you can vary the size of the planter (fig. 1).

Fig. 1

2. Place the clay on the covered cutting board and roll out a slab ¼ inch thick. Use the wood strips for guides and the rolling pin or dowel for rolling out the clay (fig. 2).

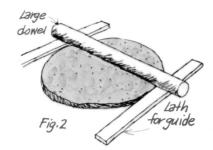

Large dowel

Lath for guide

Fig. 2

3. Place the paper pattern over the slab and cut out the shape, using a table knife.

4. With your hands, roll out 6 clay coils, each about ½ inch in diameter. Use the remaining clay for these coils.

5. Attach a coil to each side of the base, using your fingers to work the edges of the coil into the base (fig. 3).

Fig. 3

6. Starting at the bottom, lay a short coil across the end, joining it to the base with your fingers.

7. Add the next coil above the first, overlapping it about ¼ inch. Pinch the coils together on the outside edge with your thumb. Smooth the inside with your fingers, working from the bottom to the top and taking care to close all cracks (fig. 4).

How to make

1. With a table saw, cut the 2 by 2 into four 22-inch lengths and eight 20-inch lengths.

2. With a table saw, cut 45° angles at the ends of the four 22-inch 2 by 2s. Form a mitered square and join with nails. This will be the center square. Angle the eight 20-inch 2 by 2s and join to form two 20-inch squares (fig. 1).

3. Nail the 2 small frames on either side of the large one (fig. 2).

4. Cut 2 triangular side panels from the 1-inch-thick wood and nail them in place (figs. 2 and 3).

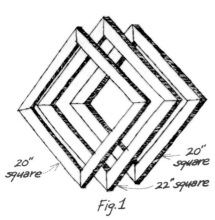

20" square
20" square
22" square

Fig. 1

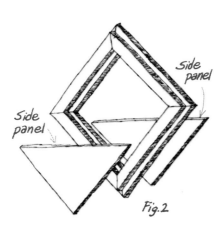

Side panel
Side panel

Fig. 2

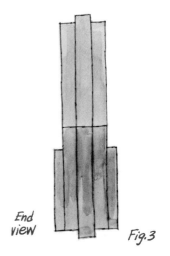

End view

Fig. 3

5. To minimize water stains, apply several coats of polyurethane varnish.

8. As the work progresses, stuff the completed portion with crushed paper towels to retain the expanding shape of the planter.

9. When the coils reach the top, smooth all joints.

10. Make a hole (for hanging the planter) in the center back with a knitting needle, ½ inch from the top. If you want a drainage hole in the bottom of the planter, use a copper penny as a pattern and cut a hole at the bottom with the knife.

11. Let the pot dry for several hours. When the pot is stiff enough to handle, use the table knife to trim excess clay from the sides.

12. Finish the piece by glazing and firing according to the requirements of the clay and glaze.

Fig. 4

Rippled surface *of wall planter results from pinching clay coils together. Design: Mary Helen Chappell.*

Containers from Nature

Plants on the Half Shell

Handpainted eggshell *is snug home for small plant. Design: Anne Easley.*

Nature's grandest "containers" are rock crevices, lush forest floors, and arid desert canyons. And you can capsulize these super-scale plant worlds within the confines of a handcrafted plant container.

Plants artfully blend with elements of nature: stones, sand, wood, reeds, gourds, shells. Some of these natural containers—shells and gourds, for example—are ready for planting without any preparation or alterations. Other containers use such natural elements as reeds and pebbles incorporated into the design and held in place by adhesives or molded into different shapes.

Most containers made from natural materials have the special shortcoming of organic matter: they tend to deteriorate at a faster rate than containers made from clay, metal, or plastic. A waterproof sealant (polyurethane varnish) will help prevent decay of the organic material.

Additional natural materials you can try are:
- Woven grass or pine needles
- Redwood burls
- Small pebbles set in resin mold
- Colorful desert sands, glued to wood
- Acorn caps glued to wood planter

Containers supplied by nature produce harmonizing, integrated designs that greatly enhance living plants. The smooth, perfect shape of an egg makes a simple, elegant container for very small house plants or cuttings.

Though a plain, unadorned egg has a natural beauty of its own, you may want to improve on nature by painting or drawing on the egg. If so, keep the design simple and remember that a cascading plant, a plant sling, or egg holder will obscure the design.

Suspend the egg planter by a petite macramé sling or set it in a napkin ring, a collar made from paper, or a nest made of reeds and twigs. After being treated with polyurethane varnish, the egg should last for several years without deteriorating at the base or upper edges.

When caring for your plant, add only small amounts of water at regular intervals. You may choose to set your eggshell planter in a holder and place it on a window sill. Egg stands and egg cups are also effective ways to display the planter.

Materials and tools

1 egg (chicken, duck, turkey, ostrich)
Polyurethane varnish
Soap/water
Paper clip
Paper towel
Coloring materials: artists' pens, felt-tipped pens, acrylic paints, water colors, oils, dampened colored pencils
Nylon packing string or embroidery yarn for hanger (optional)
Push pin
Pencil
Manicure scissors
Hanging or displaying material

How to make

1. Choose an egg with no visible cracks or holes. Clean the egg in soapy water, scrubbing with a small brush if necessary. Set on a paper towel to dry.

2. With a pencil, make a circle for the opening in the top of the shell. Hold the egg in the cup of your hand and carefully make a small hole in the center of the circle with a push pin and your fingers. Carefully chip away the shell until you reach the line for the circle (fig. 1). For an even edge, use manicure scissors, cutting a spiral until you reach the line. Empty the egg into a bowl and rinse the inside of the shell. Save the chipped eggshell for use in the potting soil.

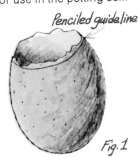

Penciled guideline

Fig. 1

3. If you decide to decorate your planter, mark your design lightly in pencil and then fill in with whatever coloring materials you've chosen (fig. 2).

Fig. 2

4. Polyurethane varnish will harden and protect your planter. Make a drainage hole in the bottom of the shell with a push pin. Twist a paper clip to form a temporary holder for the egg (fig. 3). Insert the holder and stuff the shell with a small piece of paper toweling around the wire. The toweling holds the egg and the holder in a stable position during dipping.

Bent paper clip

Fig. 3

5. Carefully dip the egg in the can of polyurethane varnish and let the excess varnish drip off. Hang the egg by the holder and let dry. Pour some varnish into the egg, coat the inside, and let dry.

6. Small house plants grow well in eggshell planters. Choose a plant that will stay small and enhance the shape of the egg—miniature ivy, wandering Jew, or bridal veil are good choices. Place the leftover shell particles in the bottom of the shell planter. With a teaspoon, add a small amount of potting soil, making a cavity for the plant. Insert the plant and cover the roots with more soil. Water sparingly (fig. 4).

Ceramic ring to hold egg

Fig. 4

Rustic Box of Wood Rounds

Slices of wood set in a resin base form two sides of this planter; plain, unfinished redwood makes the other two sides. The type of wood you choose to yield wood rounds is up to your imagination—we used rounds cut from a limb of an old apple tree. The cracks, textures, and patterns are created by the wood's exposure to the elements.

Try different kinds of wood: gnarled branches, dowels, ax handles, redwood, hardwoods. The more weathered the wood, the more variety of color and pattern. You can also experiment with sizes and arrangements of wood rounds—from small circles to large ones. Or change from circular to angular shapes.

You can plant directly in the wood round planter if you drill a drainage hole in its bottom. Otherwise, make the box a size that will accommodate a standard commercial pot.

Materials and tools

2 feet of 1 by 8 redwood
Scrap plywood, about 10 by 24 inches
Wood for wood rounds (amount varies according to size of rounds, size of planter)
36 inches of 1 by 1 wood strips
White glue (water soluble)
Sandpaper
1 foot of ¼-inch wood doweling
Fiberglass resin
Resin coloring (optional)
Clear vinyl wrap
Masking tape
Brown wrapping paper
Table saw

How to make

1. To construct the wood round panels, make 1 large panel and cut in 2 pieces for the 2 sides.

a. Place clear vinyl wrap on the piece of scrap plywood and tape securely on all edges using masking tape.

b. Place brown paper over vinyl wrap and tape as you did in step a.

c. With a table saw, cut a ¼-inch rabbet into 1 side of the wood strip; then cut the strips into two 11-inch pieces and two 6-inch pieces. Apply glue to the faces of the strips and place on the covered plywood, rabbets facing up and inward (fig. 1).

d. Arrange ¼-inch-thick wood rounds inside the rectangle formed

Inlaid in a bed of resin, slices of wood form two sides of planter; rough redwood forms other sides. Design: Terry Spilsted.

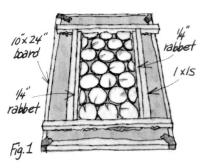

Fig. 1

10" x 24" board
1/4" rabbet
1/4" rabbet
1 x 15

by the wood strips. Glue them down, making sure the glue covers the face of each disc completely. Let dry.

e. Mix the resin according to the instructions on the box. Follow directions precisely—any variations will affect the consistency of the resin. Add desired color to resin. Work outdoors—resin fumes can be dangerous. Wear gloves.

f. Pour resin between the wood rounds first; then cover the area to a depth of 1/4 inch above the wood rounds (fig. 2).

g. Allow the resin to cure completely so the slab is not tacky but has a hard, firm surface.

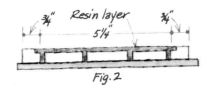

3/4" Resin layer 3/4"
5 1/4"

Fig. 2

h. Lift the slab from the surface and turn it over. Sand or file off the brown paper until the surface is clean.

i. With a saw, cut the panel into 2 pieces, each 5 1/4 inches long.

2. Attach the panels to the 2 redwood sides.

a. With a saw, cut from the redwood two 7 3/4-inch pieces; then cut 1 piece for the bottom of the planter (cut the wood to fit the inside of the assembled planter so that the piece will rest on the lower lip of the panels).

b. Cut a 3/4-inch wide-dado groove down each side of the two 7 3/4-inch pieces, 3/16 inch in from the edge.

c. Slide the 2 panels into the grooves in the redwood. With a 1/4-inch drill bit, drill 4 holes, 1 inch deep, on each side. Cut the doweling into 8 pieces, each 7/8 inch long. Put glue in the holes and hammer the doweling into place (fig. 3).

3. Insert the bottom piece and drill holes, if desired.

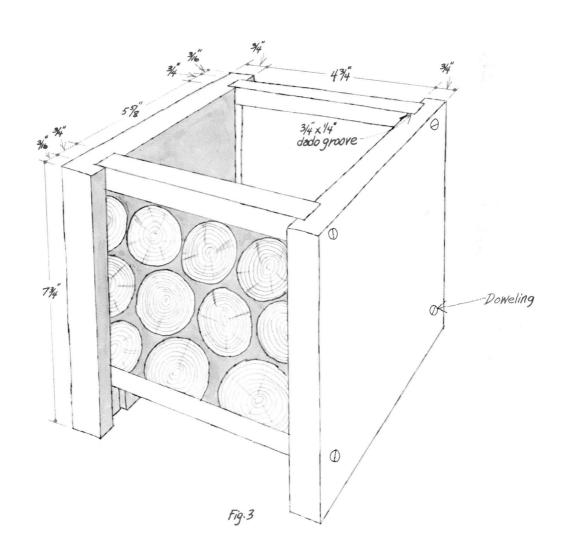

3/4"
3/16"
3/4"
3/4"
4 3/4"
3/4"
5 5/8"
3/4"
3/16"
3/4" x 1/4" dado groove
7 3/4"
Doweling

Fig. 3

Porous Planter of Pumice

The percolative power of the pumice stone makes it a perfect outdoor planter. The stone's sievelike construction allows water to pass directly through it. You can water the container and the plant at the same time—the water will transfer from the stone to the roots in the soil.

Water often and generously—because the stone is so porous, it dries out quickly.

Coarse pumice used for this planter is found in many volcanic areas throughout the western United States. The most accessible sources are stone yards and landscaping companies.

Choose a handsomely shaped piece, the larger the better. Since it's full of holes, a pumice stone weighs much less than an ordinary stone of the same size.

Materials and tools

Pumice
Hammer
Chisel
Spoon
Old ax

How to make

1. Level the bottom of the stone with an old ax.
2. Plan the size and number of holes desired for planting.
3. With a hammer, chisel, and spoon, gouge out the holes. Use the spoon to remove the pumice particles as you work (fig. 1).

Fig. 1

4. Plant the holes, using a soil mix with good drainage: 1 part coarse sand, 2 parts fertile garden loam (fig. 2). The plant roots will eventually work down from the pockets of soil into the tiny, hollow channels in the rock.

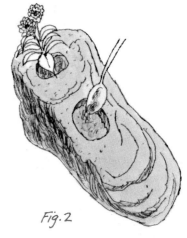

Fig. 2

5. Water daily and use a liquid fertilizer occasionally. In a shady location, moss will develop on the stone.

Shells - the Ocean's Natural Vessel

The natural shapes of seashells make jewel-like containers for small plants. You'll discover that the rounded, graceful lines of some kinds of shells can accentuate a hanging plant's cascading shape or that the spiny aspect of other shells can harmonize with an elongated, delicate plant.

A shell provides its own drainage through its cracks or holes. Since the abalone shell has the most exaggerated holes for drainage, it is a good container for cuttings or for starting plants from seeds. Abalones come in almost any size.

A shell planter is attractive when suspended by a hanger or displayed on a stand. Good materials to experiment with are wire, metal strips, macramé cord, string, fishing line, hemp. Because of the small planting area, shell planters won't need a drink very often; test the soil before watering. Feed occasionally and sparingly.

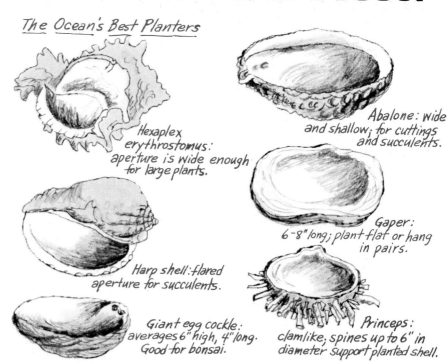

The Ocean's Best Planters

Hexaplex erythrostomus: aperture is wide enough for large plants.

Abalone: wide and shallow; for cuttings and succulents.

Harp shell: flared aperture for succulents.

Gaper: 6-8" long; plant flat or hang in pairs.

Giant egg cockle: averages 6" high, 4" long. Good for bonsai.

Princeps: clamlike; spines up to 6" in diameter support planted shell.

Pumice stone *lifts pansies a foot above ground level while showing its own and flowers' interesting contours.*

Trio of abalone shells *cradles hens and chicks (left), bedding begonia (center), and star-of-Bethlehem (right). Holes near edge of shell are natural hanging points.*

Lightning whelk *rests on copper stand. Small begonia needs little soil, watering. Design: John B. Sallemi.*

Rugged Driftwood Planter

A rugged, unrefined piece of driftwood with a plant growing from it can form a focal point and fill a void in your garden or patio. But it takes little time and effort to adapt a large piece of driftwood into a suitable plant container.

Ordinary watering in a driftwood container with no drainage might eliminate oxygen and make the soil go sour. The way to avoid this is to water by misting. This prevents overwatering and, at the same time, encourages growth of algae and moss, giving the wood an aged, oriental appearance. To fertilize, directly apply a diluted solution of fish emulsion.

Materials and tools

Driftwood
Carpenter's chisel/hammer
Household bleach

How to make

1. Find a simple, attractive piece of driftwood. After winter storms, almost any beach can yield good specimens. Ideally, the driftwood you choose should have a fair-size recess in it.

2. With a carpenter's chisel, you can enlarge the recess into a planting hole at least the size of a person's fist (fig. 1).

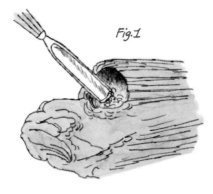

Fig. 1

3. Bleach the driftwood by washing it with a solution of household bleach and water. In addition to enhancing its appearance, this helps to eliminate any "fishy" smell.

4. Fill the cavity with a commercial outdoor planting or potting soil.

Select a plant that will trail nicely and do well when tightly root bound. In a sunny location, you might consider using a succulent—such as a small-leafed sedum, or an ice plant—or a small juniper. (fig. 2). You can also use Sprenger asparagus, a good choice in sun or shade.

Two Ideas for Ways to Plant in Driftwood

Fig. 2

Plants Growing in Stone

Defying the laws of nature, these plants seem to grow out of rock. Achieve this curious effect by slicing apart weathered rocks from the beach or mountains, taking out a center section, and then reassembling the rest of the rock.

To heighten the color of the rock, you can coat the finished planter with a water sealant or a slate-dressing preparation.

Since the planting area is small, remember to water sparingly and fertilize in small doses. Cuttings and succulents work best.

Materials and tools

Rocks
Diamond saw
Epoxy filler with
   catalyst
Chalk
Paper cup/kitchen knife
Paper towels
Poster-color paints

How to make

1. Making this planter requires 6 cuts on a diamond saw. The first cut levels the base. The next cut takes off a slab that will serve as a base layer for the upper section from which you will cut the core. The third cut takes off 1 side. Cuts 4, 5, and 6 are made around a rectangular core (fig. 1).

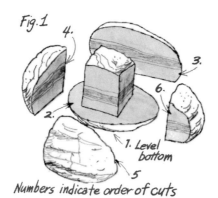

Fig. 1

Numbers indicate order of cuts

As you make the cuts, number the pieces that will stand on the base and place them in position; otherwise the contours may be difficult to match up.

2. Use the epoxy as an adhesive. The epoxy should include a hardener (catalyst) in a separate container to be added when you're ready to use the epoxy. You can approximate the color of the rock by adding dry poster-color pigment to the epoxy. (Do this before adding the catalyst, so you will have time to mix before the epoxy hardens.)

Mix the epoxy in a paper cup with a kitchen knife. After adding the catalyst, apply the epoxy in a ¼-inch-thick layer to the surface to be joined. Assemble all sections except the core and allow the epoxy to harden. You can wipe off any epoxy from the surface before it hardens.

3. To plant, mix soil with some charcoal. Water sparingly. Use plant food in small amounts applied with an eyedropper.

Hollowed-out place *near the top of 3-foot-high driftwood holds fern within natural lines of wood.*

Rough rock, *ocean and river-washed boulders, sliced apart and reassembled without rectangular core, make natural planters. Design: Mrs. Howard Quinan.*

Rattan reeds *weave together to make natural-looking containers; neutral color blends with almost any decor.*

Woven Splints and Rushes

Natural woven baskets add warmth and texture to house plants. Weaving your own baskets isn't difficult, and it allows you to experiment with different shapes and types of reeds.

Rattan reeds (from rattan palms) used for weaving are available in two shapes—round and flat—and in several sizes, each numbered according to thickness. Bundles of reeds can be purchased at some hobby shops and chair caning stores. The quantities listed below will make 4 baskets for 8-inch pots.

Materials and tools

Rattan reeds as follows:
1 bundle of #6 round reeds (for spokes)
1 bundle of #4 round reeds (for weavers)
1 bundle of ½-inch flat reeds

(Continued in next column)

Scissors
Tub of water
Plastic spray
Awl (or knitting needle or skewer)

How to make

1. Reeds must be flexible during weaving; otherwise they'll splinter and break. To soften reeds, soak them in water for 15 minutes to an hour, depending on the dryness and thickness of the reeds. As you're weaving, reeds will dry out and begin to splinter. When this happens, place your basket-to-be in water until the reeds become pliant again. Ten minutes should be long enough, but leaving it overnight won't do any harm.

2. You need 8 long spokes and 1 short spoke—the finished basket measures 10½ inches tall and 9½ inches in diameter. To compute the length of each long spoke, double the proposed basket height, add the width, and then add 8 more inches for a border at the top; each long spoke should be 38½ inches long. The short spoke should be half the length of the long spokes plus 3 inches—22¼ inches long.

3. Using a #4 round weaver, lash the spokes together and spread them an equal distance from one another so the weaving will develop symmetrically (fig. 1).

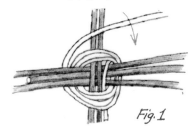

Fig. 1

4. Weave over and under spokes, using the awl as needed to open the spaces between the spokes, making weaving easier. When you reach the end of the first weaver, finish off as shown in figure 2. Begin the next weaver as shown in figure 3.

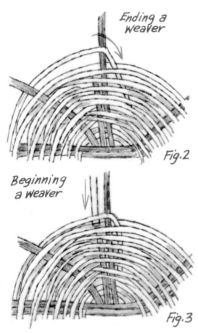

Ending a weaver

Fig. 2

Beginning a weaver

Fig. 3

5. Continue weaving until basket's base measures 9½ inches.

6. Pull the weaver you're using tight and bend the spokes to form a basket shape. Place a flower pot on the base and continue weaving loosely around the pot with a round weaver.

7. To add a flat weaver to a round, weave it around the spokes, leaving a 2-inch tail inside the basket; weave the tail into the next row (fig. 4).

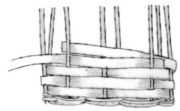

Adding a flat weaver   *Fig. 4*

8. The best woven basket will have a base that pops up slightly in the center, causing the basket to rest on its outer edge. You achieve this by: a) pressing the base into a dome shape while weaving; b) keeping the distances between spokes as nearly equal as possible; and c) keeping weavers perpendicular to spokes.

If you think the base you're weaving feels weak, you can easily add more spokes to stabilize it. When the basket's base is the desired width, triple the number of spokes by inserting a new spoke on each side of each original spoke; just slide them between the weavers.

9. Complete the basket by intertwining the spokes to secure the top edge and to form a border.

10. To make a loop border, cut the spoke ends to a uniform length (at least 5 inches) and then poke the ends down along the spokes (fig. 5).

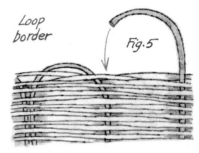

Loop border   *Fig. 5*

11. After you've finished weaving and the basket is thoroughly dry, apply a protective coat of plastic spray to prevent stains and to strengthen the basket.

Waterproofing Baskets

Watering plants in baskets can be tricky. You can line the basket with a plastic bag or aluminum foil, but the bag usually breaks and the foil tears. The best answer is to coat the basket's interior with polyester resin and newspapers. This makes the basket both waterproof and rot-resistant.

Materials and tools

Basket
Clear polyester resin and hardener
Brush
Acetone (for cleaning the brush)
Newspapers
Plastic gloves

How to make

1. Cut the newspaper in 4-inch-wide strips about 10 inches longer than the basket's diameter (the strips are to cover the bottom and extend up about 5 inches on each side). Work outdoors—the resin fumes are

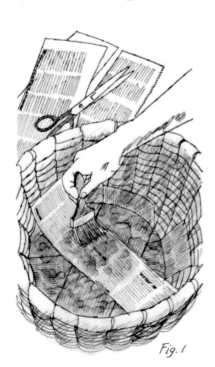

Fig. 1

dangerous as well as strong-smelling. Use gloves when working with the resin.

2. Thoroughly mix the resin with the hardener according to the directions on the can. Brush the mixture on the basket bottom and up the sides; do this sparingly to avoid having resin seep through the basket. Place strips of newspaper to cover the resin. Continue to alternate resin and paper strips (crisscrossing the strips to cover the bottom) until you have about 8 layers of paper and 8 of resin (fig. 1).

3. Pour the remaining resin into the basket, brush to cover paper strips, and let it harden. Check to be sure you have a complete seal. If there's any leakage when you pour in water, let it dry; then mix up some more resin and recoat.

4. Put a layer of crushed rock or pebbles (about 1 to 2 inches deep) in the basket. Place the plant, in its clay pot, directly on the rock or the pebbles.

Gourds for Plants

The roots of the gourd reach far back into history—farther than any other fruit. It was the first crop cultivated by early man.

Gourds have international fame as containers. They're wine bottles in Japan, herb boxes in Peru, drinking cups in Brazil. Recognized in North America more as an art form, gourds are fast becoming popular as plant containers.

A gourd is made up of cellular air pockets that act as insulation, helping to keep the soil temperature constant. When this happens the plant's growth is stimulated. Gourds have aesthetic value, too—their colors, textures, and irregular shapes complement the natural essence of the growing plant.

Materials and tools

Gourd
Spoon
Putty knife
Sandpaper
1 pound paraffin
Plastic spray sealer
Leather dye (optional)
Rags
Scouring pad

How to make

1. Soak the gourd in water overnight. Remove all outside peel with a scouring pad (fig. 1).

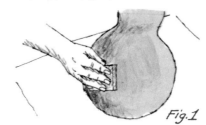

Fig. 1

2. With a putty knife, cut planting holes in the gourd and remove all seeds and membrane (fig. 2).

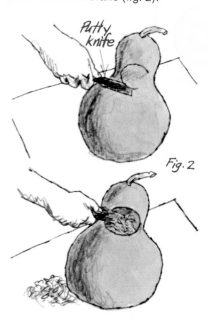

Fig. 2

Plant a Coconut Shell

The brown, furry shell that contains the sweet meat of the coconut makes a durable plant container. Cutting the shell into two pieces and joining them end to end creates a bowl-like container with its own pedestal. Nature provides the drainage holes.

Try a variation on the same idea by using each of the two halves as a container in a macramé hanger.

Materials and tools

1 coconut
Handsaw with fine teeth
Drill / ¼-inch bit
1 nail, any size
File or rasp
Kitchen knife
Rubber cement
One #8 half-inch brass screw/
    screwdriver

How to make

1. Choose a medium-size coconut. With a nail, pierce the softest of the 3 eyes on the pointed end of the coconut (fig. 1). Drain the coconut milk from the small hole.
2. With a handsaw, cut the top fourth off of the other end of the

Fig. 1

coconut—the end opposite the eye (fig. 2).

Fig. 2

3. With a kitchen knife, slice through the meat at ⅛-inch intervals (fig. 3).

Fig. 3

4. Carefully lift out the meat so that only the clean shell remains.
5. Drill ¼-inch holes through the 3 eyes (fig. 4).

Fig. 4

6. Gripping the coconut firmly, file both pointed ends of the coconut until there are even, flat surfaces on both halves (fig. 5).

Fig. 5

7. Coat both flat surfaces with rubber cement and wait until the glue is almost dry. Drill a hole from one half to the other. Join the 2 halves with a small brass screw (fig. 6).

Fig. 6

8. Plant directly in the shell, using gravel on the bottom to insure proper drainage.

3. Sand all cut edges until smooth.

4. Melt the paraffin in a double boiler or in a coffee can placed in an electric skillet.

5. Pour paraffin into the gourd cavity and swish it around until all interior surfaces are coated. The bottom part of the gourd should be especially well coated.

6. If you prefer to give your gourd a darker color, rub the exterior with a commercial leather dye. (Leather craft stores have a variety of shades. For tints, use paints, shoe polish, wood stains, diluted food coloring.)

7. Spray the outside of the gourd with plastic spray sealer. (Shellac or varnish will also work well; apply with a brush.)

8. Because this planter has no drainage, use gravel or vermiculite and charcoal with the potting soil.

9. Hang your planted gourd by attaching hemp, macramé cord, or leather thong to the gourd with an eyebolt.

Openings in a gourd *release cascades of wandering Jew. Exterior is made dark brown with leather dye, then liberally coated with clear varnish.*

Fibrous coconut shell *is home for small Swedish ivy cutting. Design: Doug Diebolt.*

Coiled Clay Container

Coils of clay wound in circles create a conical container for outdoor plants. The clay takes on a pleasingly rippled surface as your fingers pinch the coils together. The top of the container is shaped to convey an oriental feeling.

Small conifers and maple trees go well with this container; so do plants that spill over and between the cut-outs in the rim—Sprenger asparagus, English ivy, ivy geranium would be good choices.

Materials and tools

50 pounds clay with plenty of grog or sand
2 by 2-foot piece of plywood covered with canvas
Two 18-inch pieces of ¼ by 1½-inch lath
Table knife
Rolling pin or large dowel

How to make

1. Place the pieces of lath on the plywood board 14 inches apart, parallel to each other. Roll out a clay slab ¼ inch thick, using the lath as guides for the rolling pin (fig. 1).

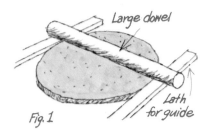

Large dowel

Fig. 1

Lath for guide

2. With a knife, cut out a circle 12 inches in diameter. Cut a drainage hole in the center, if desired.

3. Using the palms of your hands, roll out 12 to 20 coils, each about 12 inches long and ½ inch thick. (The number of coils depends on how high you want the finished container to be.) Keep the finished coils covered with a piece of plastic or a damp towel while you are working.

4. Wind the first coil around the circle; add a second coil just inside the first coil to reinforce the bottom (fig. 2). Pinch the coils between thumbs and fingers, working with thumbs on the outside. Smooth the inside coil into the bottom coil, eliminating any cracks.

Fig. 2

5. Begin building the sides by adding 1 coil inside the other, overlapping ¼ inch. Pinch the coils together as you work (fig. 3). After adding several coils, smooth the inside of the pot with your thumbs and fingers. Blend coils together until the sides are of uniform thickness. Patch thin spots with extra clay (fig. 4).

Fig. 3

Fig. 4

6. Flare the pot slightly near the top. Make the rim by adding 4 sections of short coils until desired form is achieved (fig. 5). (If your work is interrupted, cover the pot with plastic sheeting to prevent drying.)

Fig. 5

7. Glaze the pot for color and texture. Fire according to the requirements of the clay and type of glaze. Arrange to have firing done by a ceramics dealer if you don't have a kiln.

Containers used outdoors must stand up to rain, extreme temperatures, and the bleaching, hot sun. Outdoor planters must be built of sturdy stuff.

Among woods, redwood and cedar are the most durable. Other woods such as fir and pine may be used if the finished planter is coated with a protective wood sealer.

Select materials for outdoor planters to withstand harsh weather. Nails must be galvanized; glue must be waterproof. Avoid rope or hemp unless you're willing to replace them periodically.

Containers filled with plants play several outdoor roles: they are decorative elements for decks or patios; miniature gardens for apartment and condominium dwellers; substitute garden areas where clay or sandy soil is a problem.

You can plant directly inside an outdoor planter. Use pot shards and gravel for drainage. If you prefer to slip a nursery can or pot inside, raise it off the bottom of the container with rocks or gravel.

Dimpled surface *of container creates light patterns. Design: Mary Helen Chappell.*

Living Walls

Soft, framed cushions of moss make decorative wall hangings for plants. Outdoor patio walls and garden fences are natural palettes for these artistic strokes of greenery.

Moss frames have modest needs: a fine mist watering once or twice a week, occasional fertilizing, sunlight, trimming when necessary, and rotating every few days when stems begin to turn. Succulents are the best plants for these cushions.

Materials and tools

44 inches of thick reed
Epoxy glue
Catalyst for epoxy
Straight pins
Scissors
½ yard of soft fiberglass
   screening, 36 inches wide
Heavy nylon thread/sewing needle
Sphagnum moss
¼-inch upholstery tacks/hammer
Galvanized wire
Wall hooks for hanging

How to make

1. Cut 2 circles of screening, each 14 inches in diameter.
2. With the nylon thread and a needle, sew the edges of the circles together, leaving an opening several inches long for filling (fig. 1).

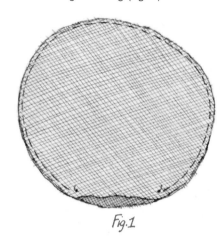

Fig.1

3. Turn inside out and fill with moss to form a firm, flat shape. Close the circle by sewing with nylon thread (fig. 2).

Fig.2

4. To make a frame, form a thick, 44-inch-long reed into a circle; pin and glue ends together (fig. 3).

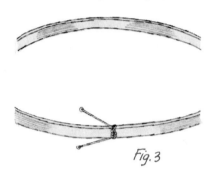

Fig. 3

The Planter That's a Cinch

Nailless, screwless *redwood planter is pulled together by four rods. Planter is easy to take apart and will not split or warp. Design: Don Ryan.*

This planter is a cinch—it's held together by four rods. No nails or screws are used, just the four threaded rods that pull the five pieces of 1 by 12 redwood together but make it easy to take apart. Because of the drilled drainage holes in the bottom, you can plant directly inside the planter.

Materials and tools

6½ feet of 1 by 12 rough
   redwood
4 galvanized, threaded 5/16-inch
   rods, each 14¼ inches long
8 hexagonal washers and nuts to
   fit the rods
Drill/⅜-inch and ¾-inch bits
Adjustable wrench
Router, table saw, or circular saw
Handsaw

How to make

1. With a handsaw, cut the 1 by 12 redwood into 5 pieces: 3 pieces 12

5. With the upholstery tacks and hammer, attach the cushion to the frame. Run a loop of wire through the cushion for hanging (fig. 4).

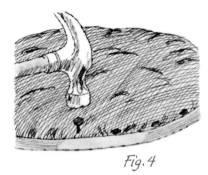

Fig. 4

6. With the framed cushion right side up, cut slashes in the screening large enough to admit the stems of the largest plant first. Wire the largest plants into the cushion to keep them secure while rooting. Add smaller succulents.

7. Lay the arrangement flat during a 2 to 3-week period outdoors in a sunny place. Mist daily. In 3 or 4 weeks, roots should be established and the frame will be ready to hang.

Living circle of succulents *framed and hung on wall goes outside on patio wall or fence. House plants can also grow in moss frame for use indoors.*

---

inches long, 2 pieces 18 inches long.

2. Make dado grooves in the 18-inch end pieces to receive the 12-inch side and bottom pieces. The grooves should be ¼ inch deep, 1 inch wide, and 12 inches long. Cut the grooves ½ inch in from the sides and 6 inches up from the bottom (fig. 1).

3. In each 18-inch piece, drill four ⅜-inch holes in the positions shown below (fig. 2).

4. Drill several ¾-inch holes in the bottom for drainage.

5. Insert and tighten the 4 rods with the nuts and washers. Be careful not to tighten them so much that you split the wood (fig. 3).

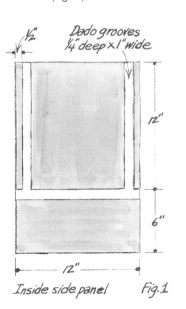

½" Dado grooves ¼ deep x 1" wide

12"

6"

12"

Inside side panel Fig. 1

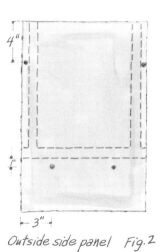

4"

1"

3"

Outside side panel Fig. 2

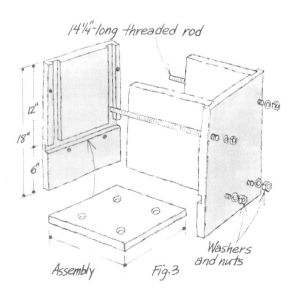

14¼"-long threaded rod

12"

18"

6"

Assembly Fig. 3

Washers and nuts

Earthen-tones *of clay bonsai planter blends with natural setting. Dwarf beach tree grows in moss-covered soil. Design: Mary Helen Chappell.*

Bonsai Planter-Simplicity

The Japanese have a reverent, sensitive perception of nature that evokes the orderly, harmonious gardens-in-miniature known as "bonsai." A bonsai container cloisters a micro-landscape that reflects nature in its totality. Bonsai is open valley, still forest, alpine scenery—all in miniature.

Because of its Lilliputian scale, bonsai is an ideal answer for the people with little or no gardening space. Decks, outdoor plant shelves, and patios are effective settings for bonsai.

Materials and tools

10 pounds of clay containing either sand or grog
2 by 2-foot piece of plywood covered with canvas
Two 18-inch pieces of ¼ by

(Continued on next page)

The Organ Pipe Planter

A congregation of multilevel planter boxes resembles an assembly of organ pipes. The design has potential for endless change: make boxes in various heights and widths, and alter the arrangement according to your mood, the types of plants, the needs of the environment.

The directions below are for one planter box of any size. Repeat the procedure for as many boxes as you want. Two procedures are listed: one requires a radial-arm saw and the other a handsaw.

Materials and tools

Clear, all-heart redwood (amount depends on box size)

(Continued on next page)

Varied arrangements *of modules average 4 feet tall. Design: Greg Smith.*

. . . Materials and tools (cont'd.)

1½-inch lath
Table knife
Paring knife or ice pick
Ruler
Rolling pin or large dowel
Vinegar
Plastic sheeting
Small paint brush

How to make

1. Set aside about 2 pounds of clay and put it in a plastic bag to keep it moist. Place the rest of the clay in the center of the canvas-covered board and beat it with your palms until the clay is leveled to ½-inch thickness. Place the laths parallel to each other, about 12 inches apart. With the dowel or rolling pin, roll out the clay between the laths using the laths as guides for the roller. Work from the center until the clay slab is ¼ inch thick. Let the slab stiffen for about 4 hours (fig. 1).

2. With a ruler and knife, measure and cut out the following 5 pieces (fig. 2):
   2 sides: 1¾ by 6½ inches
   2 sides: 1¾ by 7¾ inches
   1 bottom: 6½ by 8 inches

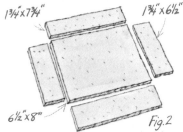

3. Using the paring knife or ice pick, score in a crisscross pattern all surfaces to be joined (fig. 3).

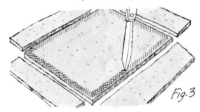

4. Assemble the planter by moistening the scored edges with vinegar and pressing the pieces together.

5. Take a piece of the reserved clay and roll out a long coil about ⅜ inch thick. Work the coil into the seam where the sides join the bottom. Reinforce the corner seams in the same manner.

6. When the pot is stiff enough to hold its shape well, turn it over and bevel the bottom edges with a table knife. Bevel or soften the corners if you like.

7. With a knife, cut 1 or more drainage holes (½ to ¾ inch in diameter) in the bottom.

8. Form the feet by bending short lengths of coil and applying them to the bottom corners. Each coil is 3½ inches long and ⅝ inch thick. Score and moisten the surfaces to be joined. With the thumb, work the ends of the coils into the bottom of the pot. Place a board over the entire surface and apply gentle pressure until the 4 feet are level (fig. 4). Glaze and fire.

. . . Materials and tools (cont'd.)

1½-inch, #8 flathead screws
Screwdriver
Pencil/ruler
30/60 triangle or protractor
Radial-arm saw or handsaw (directions for both are included)
Caulking compound or epoxy resin
Drill/⅛-inch bit

How to make

1. With a radial-arm saw:
   a. After determining the height of the planter, cut the 2 side pieces to length. The lower edge should be square and the upper edge slanted at a 30° angle (fig. 1).
   b. Measure the shorter (front) edge of the side pieces and cut the front piece to correspond. Bevel the top edge of the front piece at a 30° angle.

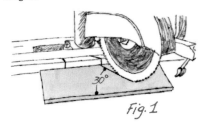

c. Drill pilot holes and attach sides to front piece with screws (fig. 2).

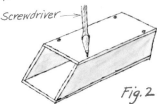

d. Measure back height from the sides already cut, adding 7/16 inch for the 30° bevel (if you're using ¾-inch-thick lumber—the thicker the lumber, the more this increases). Cut back piece to size. Drill pilot holes and attach to sides with screws.

e. With scrap from sides, cut a bottom piece to fit the interior of the planter. Place it in the planter at the desired depth and put screws through the sides, front, and back of planter to hold the bottom in place.

2. With a handsaw:
   a. Screw 4 boards of equal length together in the same manner as in the radial saw method. Be sure that the ends of the boards are flush with each other at the bottom and that the screws are not in the path of the saw cut.

b. Using a 30/60 triangle or protractor, draw a 30° angle on one side of the box at the desired height. Square the lines across the back and front of the box where the angled line intersects with the corners. Draw another angled line on the other side of the box, meeting the squared lines across the front and back. All lines are needed to keep the handsaw on a straight line.

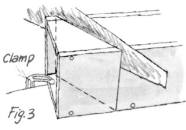

c. Lay the box on its side and cut along the pencil lines with a handsaw. Sand the cut edges (fig. 3).

3. You can fill each box with soil or place a pot inside. If you plant directly in the planter, caulk the seams or seal the interior with epoxy resin and drill drainage holes. If you use pots, be sure to place saucers under the pots or, if you prefer, caulk or seal as described above.

Store Bought Facelifts

Begin with the Basic Clay Pot...

1

2

3

4

5

The most enthusiastic house plant collector may be oblivious to the untapped versatility of the clay pot, whose mundane face can assume a kaleidoscopic assortment of new guises. This least expensive, easiest-to-obtain plant container—the clay pot—needs a facelift.

Possibilities for facelifts are infinite. Have fun experimenting. What we show you in this chapter is just a sampling. Among other materials for decorating clay pots are seashells, pasta shells, leaves, sculpture wire, pebbles, sand, buttons, foil, mylar, mosaic tile, ceramic beads, seeds, felt, sequins, pen and ink, spray paint, and finger paint.

Here are some technical considerations that apply to most clay pot facelift projects. Coat the porous clay form with a clear polyurethane sealer before adding any new covering. If you want your colors to stand out, seal the pot first with a white polyurethane paint. When applying three-dimensional objects, use a waterproof glue. If you use a water soluble adhesive for collages, cover the finished project with the clear polyurethane sealer.

Glowing with results of facelifts are these 10 containers:

1. Cornhusks bound together by string and jute form woven covering that is glued to pot's surface.

2. Small squares with painted design are products of a flour, water, and salt dough that was baked and cut. Squares are glued to pot that got its color from plastic spray paint. Blue ribbon, glued around lip, is finishing touch.

3. Reed mat, cut to fit around pot, has brown twine woven through it; glue fastens mat to pot surface.

4. Pieces of fabric lend design to a pot sealed by plastic spray paint. Polymer acrylic paint is adhesive.

5. Strips of tissue paper, held on by polymer acrylic paint, are the secret of this pot's good looks.

6. Yarn motifs applied with glue decorate white plastic pot.

7. Adding texture are bits of redwood bark, glued to pot's surface.

8. Designs cut from baked dough—made colorful by polyurethane paint—trim a painted white pot. Flower shapes are glued to pot; clear plastic paint seals the whole colorful creation.

9. Hemp rope wraps around base of pot and, with brown twine interwoven, decorates lip; glue serves as adhesive.

10. Pattern created with stencils decorates a pot coated with polyurethane paint. Colors are acrylic. Clear plastic paint gives final seal.

New Glazes for New Faces

Languishing in its terra cotta world, a clay pot might never realize its potential for becoming far more dazzling or distinguished looking. But today ceramic glazes transform ordinary pots into colorful plant containers, and a bright future lies ahead for the humble clay pot.

You can find unglazed clay pots of all shapes and sizes at most garden supply shops. Be sure to select pots that are free from cracks, pebbles, and blemishes.

Ceramic glazes in a wide range of colors and finishes are sold at most ceramic or pottery supply stores. Samples of the glazes on clay show what the colors look like after firing. They are close approximations but not entirely accurate guides, since the glaze colors are affected by the color of the clay itself.

Apply glazes with a paint brush; three thick coats are needed to insure good color quality. Allow a few minutes' drying time between coats. Since the unfired glazes bear no resemblance to their fired color, keep a glaze-color brochure handy as a reminder.

Neatness and artistic skill aren't required—a casual overlapping of the colors may lead to some interesting effects.

Avoid glazing the bottoms of the pots. Otherwise, pots may stick to the kiln shelves during firing, and beads of glaze may keep pots from sitting flat. Do paint the glaze over the rim and down the inside to the expected soil level.

If pots are to be used indoors, decorate saucers in matching glazes and use them to prevent water marks

on furniture. To make sure the saucers are waterproof, glaze the insides.

Many commercial firms will fire pots (look in the Yellow Pages under Ceramics). Each will have its own price scale, based on the sizes of the pots or on kiln volume. If you intend to glaze very large pots, first make certain you'll have access to a kiln that's large enough to accommodate them. Discuss cost, too. Finally, be sure to tell the kiln operator that you used low-fire glazes. Below are 3 design suggestions for glazes.

Retrimmed Redwood Planters

Redwood planters are perfect prospects for facelifts. Anyone seeking something distinctive can modify any of the plain redwood planters available at nurseries and garden centers.

Redwood planters come in three basic types. One is the rectangular planter box offered in various lengths for use as window boxes or on patios, decks, and walls. The other two are tubs: a square box with straight or sloping sides, and the familiar octagonal container (fig. 1).

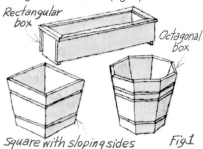

Rectangular box / *Octagonal box* / *Square with sloping sides*   Fig.1

You customize a redwood planter by adding decorative wood trim and then staining the entire planter. The only materials you'll need are redwood trim strips, galvanized nails, and a stain.

The rectangular box with straight sides is the easiest to remodel. Complete the outer frame of the box with 1 by 1s. Miter a small inner rectangle parallel to the outer frame. To avoid splitting the wood strips, drill pilot holes for the finishing nails. Nail heads can be hidden below the surface with a nail set (fig. 2). Fill the holes with wood putty.

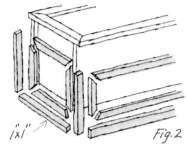

1"x1"   Fig.2

For the square box with sloping sides, use 1 by 3s. Measure the slope of the sides of the planter with a protractor. Consult a compound miter table to determine the exact bevel and miter angles for setting your miter box or power saw. Or, with a handsaw, cut each piece slightly longer than you need and file or power-sand each piece to fit.

Because box dimensions often vary, cut each piece separately as you go around the planter. Tack on the strips with nails (fig. 3).

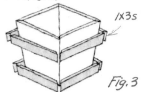

1x3s   Fig. 3

The octagonal planter takes ½ by 1¼-inch redwood trim strips. Follow the same steps as with the preceding sloping planter box to determine miter and bevel settings. Measure and fit each wood segment before going to the next one (fig. 4).

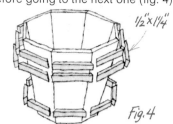

½"x1¼"   Fig.4

Finish the boxes with a semi-transparent stain. The stain helps to blend the wood of the new trim strips with that of the purchased planter.

Bright glaze *on clay pot adds new dimension to ordinary terra cotta face. Simple designs yield dramatic effects.*

Redwood strips dress up *standard rectangular containers clustered here in deck-side arrangement.*

Slip on a Cedar Sleeve

When you buy a good-size plant, it's likely to come potted in a homely gallon can. If you camouflage that can, you rid yourself of the necessity for repotting your plant into another container.

Rough-sawn cedar forms the sides of an easy-to-make sleeve for cans. Five-gallon or larger cans will fit into the sleeves and can be changed from season to season. The adjustable shelf allows containers of different sizes to be set at the ideal height for each shrub, tree, or vine.

Materials and tools

(Quantities and sizes vary
   according to size of sleeve)
1 by 12 rough-sawn cedar
2 by 2 rough-sawn cedar

(Continued in next column)

Eight ¼ by 1½-inch lag bolts
Wrench/pliers
Drill/9/16-inch bit
Nails/hammer/handsaw
Linseed oil/rags
Shelf brackets

How to make

1. With a handsaw, cut the 1 by 12 cedar into pieces that correspond to the desired height of the sleeve.

2. Cut the 2 by 2 in the same way. Refer to figure 1 for the necessary dimensions and the directions for assembly. You can build the sleeve as high as you like and assemble it with a few lag bolts in predrilled holes. The base is of 2 by 2s nailed to the bottom plate. The base and bottom plate are then nailed to the sides. When the sleeve is completed, rub the wood with linseed oil.

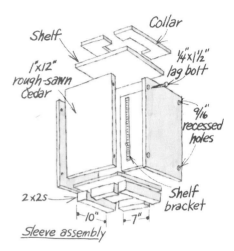

Shelf
Collar
1"x12" rough-sawn cedar
¼"x1½" lag bolt
9/16" recessed holes
Shelf bracket
2 x 2s
10"
7"
Sleeve assembly

Boutiques, *garden supply centers, crafts shops are rich sources of plant containers of every size, shape, and material.*

Elegant Store Bought Containers

A burgeoning supply of plant containers can be found in garden supply stores, department stores, gift and decorating shops, and discount stores. The choice is almost overwhelming and includes true plant containers with adequate drainage holes and saucers, as well as cachepots that need to have holes drilled in them for drainage.

Drilling holes in store bought containers is simple. Use an electric drill with a masonry bit (tungsten-carbide). Drill several ¼-inch holes rather than a single large one. Turn the pot upside down and brace the inside with a wood block. Drill from the outside in and drill very, very slowly.

When using pots without holes, layer gravel and soil, and water the plants sparingly. Or you can use such a container as a sleeve for a clay pot.

Smart-looking cedar sides are rough-sawn, cut to 12, 18, and 36-inch heights, and finished with linseed oil. They camouflage less attractive containers inside. Design: Paul Anderson.

Containers with a Foreign Flair

International collection of handsome, inexpensive plant containers, all purchased at import shops. For scale, note that shelves are a foot apart. From left to right:

Top shelf: All of these are Japanese. Light brown stoneware pot, three-piece set for bonsai, blue green ceramic container with flowering plum pattern.

Middle shelf: These are European. Yellow straw basket holding plastic liner (Italy), bright blue ceramic container (Portugal), heavy cast stone container (Spain), ceramic basket weave planter with liner (Spain).

Lowest shelf: All are Mexican. Clay pot with handpainted green swirls, improvised planter—bean pot—holds 4-inch pot with sedum, pink-flowered clay pot.

Merchandise varies from store to store, and part of the fun is shopping around. Availability also varies, but new containers are constantly being shipped to import stores.

From foreign countries come containers that convert to unusual planters.

Unique Designs
in Wood

Sandblasted wood grain of redwood cubes, see facing page, adds texture to simple lines. Corners are cut to interlock with each other, creating a design featuring contrast of wood grain. Design: John August.

What's so great about wood for plant containers? Everything.

- Wood is durable, especially if it's redwood.

- Wood is easy to drain because of its porosity and irregularities and because almost all wood containers have joints.

- Wood's organic nature blends harmoniously with any plant.

- Wood will take a stain or opaque paint. It can also be left to weather naturally.

- Wood is easy to obtain.

Wood has infinite design versatility, and this chapter is devoted to wooden planters that illustrate that versatility. The projects range from the simplest to the most difficult. Most require only simple tools; others require table saws, precise measurements, and accurate cuts. From all of them you can gain an appreciation of the flexibility of wood by seeing the various ways it's used to contain growing plants.

Design ideas in this chapter should spark your imagination and inspire you to try your hand at designing your own wood planter.

The Yin-Yang Cube

A cube such as either of those on the facing page is constructed of two complementary elements of the same shape—one is the mirror image of the other. The two elements interlock precisely, creating a cube with a zigzag pattern on the edges. The concept parallels the oriental philosophy of Yin and Yang—hot and cold, life and death. Each of the opposites is essential to the existence of the other.

The cube container works best in either of two sizes: a 4 by 4-inch cube or a 5 by 6-inch rectangle. A coating of linseed oil will protect the outside and accent the wood. Sandblasting the exterior will raise the grain and give the box a sculptured look. If you plan to sandblast, select wood with a wide, even grain pattern. In any case, choose wood that is free of knots.

The following directions are for a 4-inch cube.

Materials and tools

17 inches of 1 by 6-inch clear, all-heart redwood.
2¾-inch square of ⅜-inch exterior plywood
Sixteen 10-penny, 1½-inch threaded or cinch brass nails, galvanized/hammer
Chalk
Linseed oil, turpentine
Thick rubber band or band clamp
Pitch or roofing mastic/paint brush
Table saw
Drill/½-inch bit and a smaller bit for nail holes

Note: For uniform construction, rip the redwood to 4 inches and cut one 17-inch length for the boxes. Make sure end cuts are square.

How to make

1. Cut the 17-inch piece of redwood into four 4-inch squares. Using chalk, number them from right to left. You can use a stop block to make repeated cuts of same measurements.

2. Since all pieces are identical, cuts made on the first piece can serve as guides for cutting the other 3 pieces. Be accurate—measurement is critical. Cut a blind dado in 1 square as shown (fig. 1). Use a table saw with a stop clamped on the fence to prevent the groove from passing through the piece. The blind dado gives the box a cleaner appearance (fig. 2).

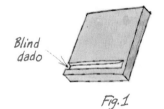

Fig. 1

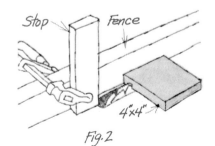

Fig. 2

3. Make the cutouts on the edges. Height of each cutout must be exactly ½ the width of the wood; depth must be exactly equal to the thickness of the wood. Measure carefully (fig. 3).

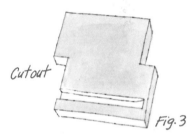

Fig. 3

4. Drill a drainage hole in the plywood bottom and insert the bottom into the dado groove of side 1. Assemble the box, proceeding in a clockwise direction with the sides in numerical order (fig. 4). After the box is assembled with the bottom in place, use a thick rubber band to hold it together.

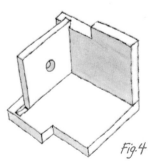

Fig. 4

5. With the drill and the small bit, predrill the nail holes.

6. Insert and hammer in nails. Mix one part linseed oil with one part turpentine and coat the outside. Coat the inside with pitch or roofing mastic before planting.

A Planter Puzzle

Interlocking parts *have notches, slots, and grooves, enabling this planter to fit together precisely without the use of screws, nails, or bolts. Design: John August.*

An interlocking planter puzzle solves a problem constantly plaguing wooden planters: being in contact with wet soil on one side, heat and dry air on the other side causes severe warping after a period of time if the structural members are held rigid by nails, bolts, or screws. With fasteners eliminated, this planter expands and contracts freely.

Follow the directions carefully in order for the parts to interlock properly. Its greatest asset is flexibility—vary the dimensions and build the planter in whatever size you like.

Materials and tools

Clear, all-heart redwood (see chart for functions, sizes, and cuts of wood)

(Continued on next page)

Lumber You'll Need

Member		Stock	Quantity to Buy	Quantity and Size After Milling
A	Top and bottom bands	2 x 2	19'	Eight 28½" lengths
B	Legs	4 x 4	8'	Four 2' lengths
C	Side panels	1 x 3	54'	Thirty-six 17½" lengths
D	Bottom braces	2 x 3	8'	Four 19" lengths
E	Bottom	1 x 12	4'	Two 20" lengths

Note—all members may need to be trimmed to fit during assembly.

Table saw or handsaw (miter
saw is optional)
Pitch or roofing mastic/paint brush
Linseed oil/turpentine/brush

How to make

1. Member A: Cut half lap joints
1½ inches from each end (fig. 1).
Assemble 2 frames. Where the pieces
cross, the members should be
perfectly flat.

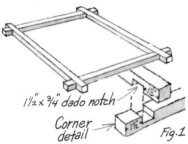

1½" x ¾" dado notch

Corner
detail

Fig. 1

2. Member B: Dado the top and
bottom outside legs to receive side
bands. Dado grooves should be ¾
inch deep and 1½ inches wide,
beginning 2 inches from the tops
and 2 inches from the bottoms
(fig. 2). Cut dadoes on lower inside
part of legs ½ inch deep and 1½
inches wide to receive leg braces
(fig. 3). Cut a dado groove on the

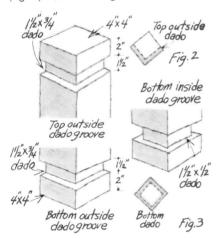

1½"x¾"
dado

4"x4"

Top outside
dado

2"
1½"

Fig. 2

Top outside
dado groove

Bottom inside
dado groove

1½"x¾"
dado

1½"
2"

1½" x ½"
dado

4"x4"

Bottom outside
dado groove

Bottom
dado

Fig. 3

inside of each leg to receive the
side panels (fig. 4). For an optional

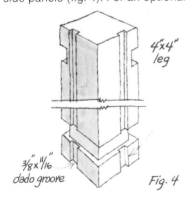

4"x4"
leg

⅜"x"/₁₆"
dado groove

Fig. 4

design detail, bevel the top of the
legs with a miter saw at a 45° angle
on all 4 sides, coming to a point
at the top (fig. 5).

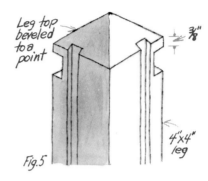

Leg top
beveled
to a
point

⅜"

4"x4"
leg

Fig. 5

3. Member C: Rabbet each edge
of each piece so they can be stacked
flush to each other. Rabbets are
unnecessary for bottom of lowest
panel and top of highest panel
(fig. 6).

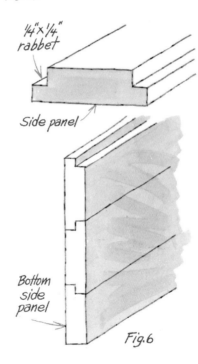

¼"x¼"
rabbet

Side panel

Bottom
side
panel

Fig. 6

4. Member D: Rip each length
to 1½ inches width. Dado each
piece to receive side panels (fig. 7).

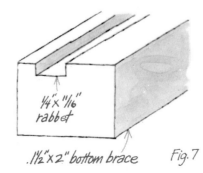

¼"x"/₁₆"
rabbet

.1½"x 2" bottom brace   Fig. 7

5. Member E: Cut the 2 pieces to
fit after entire planter is assembled.
6. Assemble all pieces:

a. Lay bands on edge to receive
dadoed legs. Legs should fit snugly
but not tightly. If fit is too tight, use
a rasp and clean out the dado. It
may be helpful to clamp legs to
bands temporarily (fig 8).

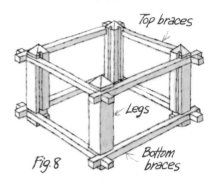

Top braces

Legs

Bottom
braces

Fig. 8

b. Stand the planter on its legs.
Check to be sure the legs are snug
against the bands. Carefully measure
openings for braces. Measurements
may vary slightly. Cut braces to fit
snugly against legs and slide them
in place (fig. 9).

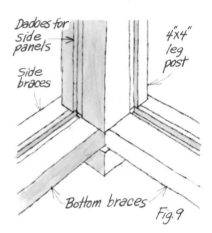

Dadoes for
side
panels

Side
braces

4"x4"
leg
post

Bottom braces   Fig. 9

c. After braces are in place,
measure the top opening for side
panels. This measurement may vary
slightly from side to side. Trim
panels so they drop in place with
a 1/32-inch clearance. The first
panel locks in the bottom brace. Trim
the top panel to end flush with the
dado in the leg.

d. Cut the 1 by 12 boards to fit
in the bottom. Notch corners to fit
around the legs. The bottom should
be a loose fit to allow for drainage.
Holes may be also drilled. The
bottom boards rest freely on the leg
braces.

7. Coat the inside with pitch.
Finish the outside with linseed oil cut
in half with turpentine.

Logs-Containers in the Raw

Plants growing out of an opening in a log may bewilder a casual observer. The openings aren't holes—the planting areas result from cutting a log apart and then putting it back together again. Suitable for use outdoors, the log planter has ample drainage and can be made with simple tools.

Materials and tools

1 bark-covered log, preferably redwood, but cedar or pine will also work.
Handsaw or chain saw
Wedge, ax handle, or hatchet
Eight 3-penny galvanized nails/hammer
Hemp rope/waterseal/scissors
Electrical staples
Drill/¼-inch bit

How to make

1. Choose a section of log that is free of knots. Cut a length equal to twice the diameter of the log.

2. Split 2 sides off the log by first scoring and then tapping each side with a wedge and hammer. Use a wedge, ax head, or hatchet blade at least 3 inches long. If only smaller ones are available, use 2 side by side (fig. 1).

3. With a chain saw or handsaw, cut about ¾ of the way through the middle section, 1 to 2 inches from each end of the log. If a handsaw is used, make a "V" at the end of each cut (fig. 2).

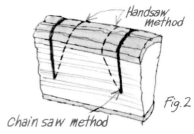

4. Using the wedge, score a line between the ends of the 2 cuts. With the hammer and wedge, split off the inside (fig. 3).

5. Tack the sides back on the log, using 4 nails at each end, 2 on the tops and bottoms (fig. 4).

The Octagon

Interlocking squares of redwood make a rustic disguise for unsightly pots. Three square frames join at the corners with notches and stack in a staggered position. Brass rods hold the pieces of wood together, eliminating the need for nails. You can finish the wood by sanding and oiling it or by sandblasting it to accentuate the grain. Or you can leave the wood to weather naturally.

Materials and tools

10 feet of 1 by 2-inch redwood
3 feet of 1½-inch redwood lath (thickness varies)
Table saw or handsaw
Drill/⅛-inch bit
Pliers
Wire cutters
Hammer

How to make

1. Cut the 1 by 2 into twelve 9¾-inch lengths.

2. Cut dado grooves in 2 bottom pieces to receive the lath (fig. 1).

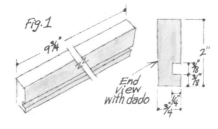

3. In all 12 pieces, cut half lap notches 1 inch deep, ¾ inch wide, and ¾ inch from each end. Make sure the notches on the 2 bottom frames are identically placed (fig. 2).

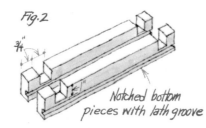
Notched bottom pieces with lath groove

4. Drill ⅛-inch holes 3¼ inches from 1 end of each piece, centering each hole. Make holes on the bottom pieces so that the holes are diagonal to each other when the lath grooves face each other (fig. 3).

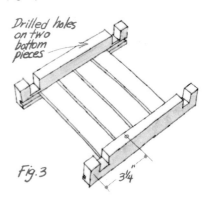

5. Cut the lath into 4 pieces, each 7 3/16 inches long.

6. Assemble the 1 by 2s in the following manner: Cut the rod into 4 equal lengths. Double over 1 end of each piece of rod ½ inch. Insert through drilled holes. Pound ends over into bottom frame. Slip the remaining frames over the wire, arranging them to gain the octagonal effect (fig. 4).

Fig. 4

6. Cut 2 lengths of hemp rope (length depends on height from which planter will hang) and waterseal them if the planter is to be used outdoors. Attach 1 end of 1 length ¾ inch in from the log's end and fasten with an electrical staple. Wrap the rope around twice, pass the end under the rope, and tack at the top (fig. 5). Repeat for the other end.

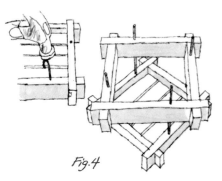

Electrical staple

Fig. 5

7. With a drill and a ¼-inch bit, drill several drainage holes in the bottom.

Insides carved out, *log has room for garden verbena. Design: Lon Merrill.*

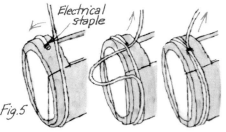

Fig. 4

7. After the third frame is added, hold 1 rod with pliers so that the lower edge of the pliers is at the midpoint of the rod. Bend the rod over so that the end meets the frame. Repeat for remaining rods (fig. 5).

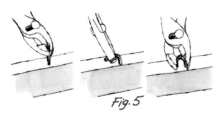

Fig. 5

8. Use the rod's loops to attach whatever hanging material you choose (macramé cord, leather, rope). Place a saucer and a pot in the planter and hang.

Grain in relief *results from sandblasting surface of redwood pieces. Hung by chain, planter holds clay pot, saucer. Design: John August.*

Sculpted Containers

Roughly rounded edges and roughly sawn redwood surfaces give these planters a naturally sculpted look. The shapes are simple to make, requiring only simple hand tools. Since the object is to arrive at a hand-hewn look, no sanding or finishing is needed; linseed oil, though, could be used to darken and to help preserve the wood.

Rough-sawn redwood varies in width—wood sizes may be adjusted to compensate.

PLANTER A

Feedbag-shaped planter *consists of five pieces of redwood. Design: Dennis Cox.*

Materials and tools

Rough-sawn redwood as follows:
  3 feet of 1 by 8
  2 feet of 1 by 10
  10 inches of 1 by 4
  Eighteen 8-penny galvanized finishing nails/hammer
  Drill/½-inch and counter-boring bits
  Wood putty/putty knife
  Handsaw
  Waterproof resorcinol glue/ brush
  Wood rasp
  Hanging material

How to make

1. With a handsaw, cut the 1 by 8 into two 16-inch lengths. Bevel both top corners of each piece. Cut the 1 by 10 into two 1-foot lengths.

2. Locate nail positions and drill countersinking holes with a counter-boring bit (fig. 1).

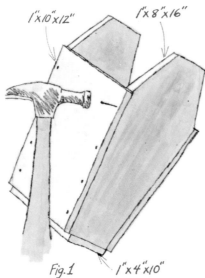

Fig. 1

3. Assemble the planter by first coating with glue all surfaces to be joined and then nailing together, countersinking the nails as you go. Use wood putty to fill nail holes (fig. 2).

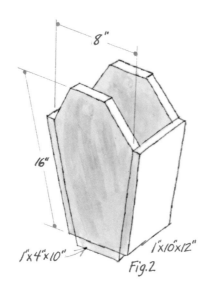

Fig. 2

4. When glue is dry, use the wood rasp to round all edges. With the drill and a ½-inch drill bit, make drainage holes in the bottom and holes on both sides at the top for hanging material. Hang with watersealed hemp rope or with chain.

Sloping sides *of low container allow plants to cascade over edges. Weathered wood enhances rough, rounded edges. Design: Dennis Cox.*

PLANTER B

Materials and tools

Rough-sawn redwood as follows:
  4 feet of 2 by 8
  6 feet of 1 by 10
  4½ feet of 2 by 2
  9 feet of 1 by 8
  Twelve 2-inch #10 galvanized screws/screwdriver
  1 foot of ¼-inch wood doweling
  Drill/¼-inch, ½-inch, and counterboring bits
  Handsaw
  Wood rasp
  Waterproof resorcinol glue/ brush

How to make

1. With a handsaw, cut the 2 by 8 into two 24-inch lengths. Bevel both ends of each piece (fig. 3). Cut the 1 by 10 into two 36-inch lengths. Cut the 2 by 2 into two 26-inch lengths. Cut the 1 by 8 into three 36-inch lengths.

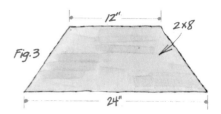

Fig. 3

Rough-sawn planter *is hexagonal shaped; five lengths of 1 by 6 redwood form sides and bottom. Design: Dennis Cox.*

2. Drill ¼-inch holes for nails, 3 at each end of the 1 by 10s (fig. 4). Then use a counterboring bit in each hole.

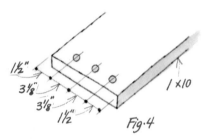

3. Assemble planter by coating with glue all surfaces to be joined and then inserting and countersinking the screws. Cut doweling to size for plugging screw holes. Glue and insert plugs. Let the glue dry.

4. With a rasp, round all edges. Use the drill and ½-inch bit to make drainage holes in the bottom (fig. 5).

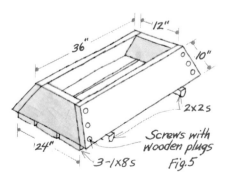

PLANTER C

Materials and tools

Rough-sawn redwood as follows:
   7½ feet of 1 by 6
   2 feet of 2 by 12
   Sixteen 2-inch #10 galvanized
     screws/screwdriver
   1 foot of ¼-inch wood
     doweling
   Drill/¼-inch, ½-inch and
     counterboring bits
   Handsaw
   Waterproof resorcinol glue/
     brush
   Wood rasp

How to make

1. With a handsaw, cut the 1 by 6 into five 17⅞-inch lengths. Cut the 2 by 12 into two 12-inch lengths.

2. Cut each 2 by 12 at angles on each side (fig. 6).

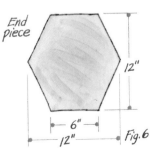

3. Drill holes for screws in 1 by 6s using a ¼-inch bit and then a counterboring bit. Two screws will go in each end of each 1 by 6 (fig. 7).

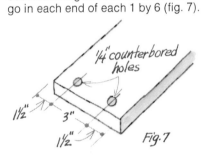

4. Assemble the box by first coating with glue all surfaces to be joined and then inserting and countersinking the screws. Cut doweling to size for plugging the screw holes. Glue and insert plugs (fig. 8).

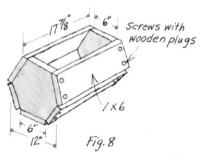

5. After the glue is dry, round all edges with a rasp. With the drill and ½-inch bit, make drainage holes in the bottom.

Built-in Planters

1

2

3

Are you looking for additional planting space? Indoors and out, you may have more room for plants than you realize. Apartments, condominiums, and homes with small living areas all have spaces with potential for growing plants.

For indoor built-in planting areas, keep these points in mind:

• Suitable temperature and light conditions are vital. Avoid drafty areas—in the path of a heat or air conditioning register, for example, plants would be exposed to excessive fluctuations of temperature. Unless the plants you want to use are able to survive prolonged heat or direct sunlight, avoid areas under skylights with a southern or western exposure; areas in front of unprotected southern or western windows; and areas near ovens, cooktops, and heaters.

Lighting should be planned to suit the needs of the specific plants. Provide for diffused light through properly oriented skylights and windows or artificial lights. Avoid locating spotlights within 3 to 4 feet of planting.

• Proper scale means more than one thing. Not only should the scale of planter and plant balance, but both should harmonize also with the scale of the furniture in the room and the size of the room itself.

• Soundness of structures is crucial if you are considering a large planter. Indoor planters must be planned with the weight of the filled planter in mind. Floors in houses are designed to support 40 pounds of live load per square foot; a cubic foot of water-soaked earth can weigh as much as 90 pounds per cubic foot.

• Moisture protection is best provided by a sheet-

(Continued on next page)

Planters within a Structure

1. A light, airy feeling is gained by the addition of this planter box within a stair railing. Before this remodeling, a solid railing kept sunlight from passing through the stairway. The new stairway has ample light to keep plants healthy, blocking the view of the bathroom from the dining area below. To maintain an open feeling from both below and above, the railing is placed low. The handrail is floated above the planter, and the back base slopes in to minimize the mass of the planter in the small hall. Planter's walls—plaster over wood framing—contain a sheet-metal box with a drain to the outside concealed in the wall (fig. 1). Design: Michael Moyer.

2. Planting area caps an overhead shelf unit, and greenery softens the angular patterns created by the oak cabinetry. Designed into the top of the unit is a sheet-metal pan that holds a layer of gravel; plants, in their separate pots, are set on the gravel for proper drainage. Plants that do well in warm kitchens include philodendron, grape ivy, and wandering Jew. It's important to avoid plants that would suffer from heat that accumulates in the upper areas of a kitchen (fig. 2). Design: Michael Moyer.

3. The outward slant of the window-pane makes space for this long, rectangular planting box. Redwood slabs frame both sides, creating a rustic bay window effect.

For water resistance, the planting box is treated with hot-mopped tar and felt. Exterior supports for the planting shelf are of redwood. Inside, lighting is built into the fascia area at the top of the window.

Such a planting area could be drained to the outside of the building. Otherwise, efficient drainage is achieved by a layer of gravel between pots and planter box.

The arrangement shown here is worth considering not only for new construction but for a remodeling, too. Most windows can be extended outward and redesigned to accommodate planting space (fig. 3). Design: Michael Leventhal, Howard Rosen.

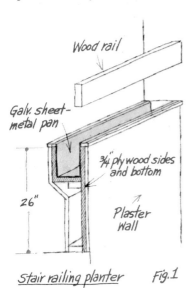

Stair railing planter   Fig. 1

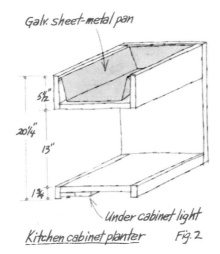

Kitchen cabinet planter   Fig. 2

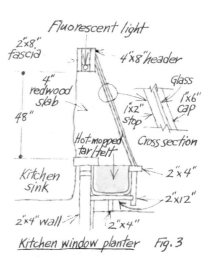

Kitchen window planter   Fig. 3

. . . Continued from page 55

Checkpoints for Built-in Planters

metal box, custom built and set into the opening. Except for very large plants, a depth of 6 to 12 inches is usually adequate. Keep the earth at least an inch below the top of the planter and layer the bottom with at least an inch of gravel for drainage. Make sure that wood and dirt are not in contact.

• The planter box should be removable for repairs. It should rest on a solid support and be fabricated from galvanized sheet metal, at least 26 gauge, with all corners soldered. The interior should be painted with asphalt emulsion or epoxy, since the natural salts, acids, or alkalies will eventually eat through the unprotected galvanizing, causing the steel to rust.

• If the location allows, install a drain to the exterior of the house or directly to the crawl space under the house. A good drainage material is flexible ½-inch PVC plastic pipe; a screen covering the end will keep bugs out.

For built-in planters, outdoors, keep these points in mind:

• If a planter is to be placed against an outside wall, building codes require a 2-inch minimum air space between the planter and wood frame wall. If the space is less than 6 inches, sheet-metal flashing is required between the planter and the wall.

• Some provision is necessary to insure that water drains away from the foundation of the house.

• Any wood in direct contact with the earth has to be all-heart redwood or wood that has been treated with a chemical wood preservative.

• The size of the planter should blend with the other landscaping elements in your garden. Choose plants that complement the planter's size, color, and texture.

• Be sensitive to the sun and shade needs of the plants you want to include. You can check Sunset's *Western Garden Book* for information.

More Ideas for Built-in Planters

Second floor landing of stairs has built-in planter where concealed metal boxes hold potted ferns. Design: Dartmond Cherk.

Stairway alcove planter has a built-in box of welded sheet metal. Design: Dartmond Cherk.

Planter box *rides the rail that separates a streetside carport from a stairway leading down to an entry. Box is constructed of redwood 2 by 4s, with plant mix held by 1 by 3s and 1 by 8s. Design: Lawrence Steiner.*

Wood and gypsum board *form outer box for this built-in planter at top of stairs. Sheet-metal planter box sits inside and holds pots of dracaena, kangaroo tree-bine, and threadleaf false aralia. Design: Sabin O'Neal Mitchell.*

Clay, ceramic, or plastic pots *rest on wood scraps, stones for extra height and drainage. Lip of sheet-metal box fits inside wood molding of built-in planter. Design: Sabin O'Neal Mitchell.*

Pipe Elbow Planter

From a pure, functional shape such as a pipe elbow section comes a multitude of possibilities. Inverted, upturned, attached to one another, hung from walls—the elbow shape can be used as a container from almost any angle. Pipe elbows are available in metal, plastic, and clay. You can plant directly inside one if you insert a platform or bottom, or you can use the elbow as a pot holder. Paint the pipe elbow or leave it natural.

Materials and tools

2 sections of 4-inch-diameter 90°
   pipe elbow
4 feet of 1 by 6 fir
Electrical socket, side tab
Line switch
10 feet of lamp cord
Electrical plug
''L'' bracket
Six 1½-inch #10 screws
Plastic spray paint (any color)
Eight 2-penny galvanized nails/
   hammer
Two ¾-inch #11 screws/screw-
   driver
¼-inch-diameter bolt, 1½
   inches long
Wall hanger
Drill/¾-inch bit and hole cutter
Handsaw
Saber saw or jigsaw
Table saw
Compass
Ruler
Pencil
Light bulb, 30-watt spot reflector,
   or fluorescent growth bulb

How to make

1. With a handsaw, cut one 30-inch length from the 1 by 6. Locate centers 4¾ inches from each end. Draw a 4-inch-diameter circle around each center, using a compass (fig. 1).

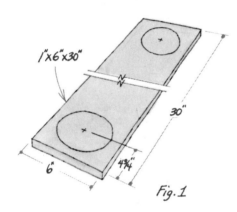

Fig. 1

2. With a compass, draw a rounded edge at each end of the 1 by 6, using the established center points. Cut the rounded ends with the saber saw (fig. 2).

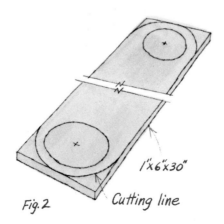

Fig. 2   Cutting line

3. With a table saw, kerf the center back ⅛ inch deep the length of the 1 by 6 for the lamp cord.

4. Trim 2 pieces of 1 by 6 to fit snugly inside the narrow end of each pipe elbow; do this by cutting the corners at 45° angles (fig. 3).

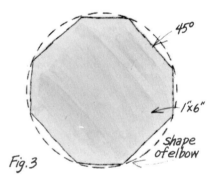

Fig. 3

5. Drill a ¼-inch hole in the mounting block for the cord above the bracket. With a hole cutter bit, drill a hole in the 1 by 6 to receive the cord where the pipe elbow will be located on the upper part of the 1 by 6. Cut 1 arm of the ''L'' bracket to ⅓ its length. Locate and screw the bracket, socket, and cord to 1 mounting block (fig. 4).

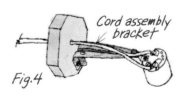

Cord assembly bracket

Fig. 4

A teakettle isn't just a teakettle—it's a potential plant container. Neither are flue tiles only for fireplaces—they can just as well be effective containers for outdoor plants.

The most mundane object can be quickly transformed into an attractive, original plant container. Utilitarian containers found in kitchens, garages, antique shops, or building supply stores are prime candidates for such use.

Ideas in this chapter should help to make you aware of plant containers that exist in your everyday environment.

Your kitchen offers terrines, baking pans, goblets, colanders, teapots, and strainers. Other areas in and around your home might reveal paint cans, garbage cans, baskets, pipe elbows, bricks, or flue pipes. With a little creativity and a lot of inspiration, these objects can be ready to plant within minutes.

Check first for drainage. Some found objects will be suitable only as decorative sleeves for clay or plastic pots. Others can be drilled for drainage (see page 44). If you want to plant directly in a container without drainage, remember to use plenty of gravel, charcoal, and vermiculite under the potting soil.

6. Fit both mounting blocks into the pipe elbows and nail them in place, using 4 nails for each (fig. 5).

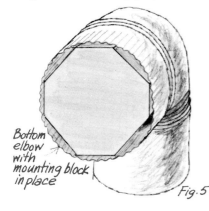

Bottom elbow with mounting block in place

Fig. 5

7. Place each pipe elbow with its mounting block on a 4-inch circle on the 1 by 6. Thread the cord and lamp assembly in the upper pipe elbow directed downward. Drill three ¼-inch holes from the back to the front through the 1 by 6 and the mounting block. Do this for each pipe elbow. Insert 3 screws for each pipe elbow (fig. 6).

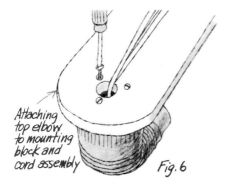

Attaching top elbow to mounting block and cord assembly

Fig. 6

8. Spray the entire unit with plastic paint. Let dry. Attach the line switch and plug. Use a 4-inch clay pot in the bottom pipe elbow and a light bulb in the top. Remove the pot to water.

Plant container-light fixture *combination gives whimsical touch to contemporary interior. Leave pipes and wood natural or paint. Design: Terry Spilsted.*

RECYCLED MATERIALS **59**

Containers from Your Kitchen

Kitchen pots and pans *make spontaneous containers for house plants in your kitchen. Bulbs grow in soil placed in chicken wire baskets made to fit pot. Basket is lined with aluminum foil to hold soil. Holes poked in foil allow drainage.*

Lettuce baskets *hold hanging herb gardens for your kitchen. Herbs in 6-inch clay pots are set in lettuce baskets suspended by chains and eye hooks; 5-inch pottery saucers fit in bottom to catch drips. Move baskets to sink for watering.*

Old-fashioned, *blue-speckled enameled steel teakettle, used as plant container, adds homespun flavor to kitchen decor.*

Cinnamon-colored *ceramic coffee pot holds fern in sandy potting mix.*

Containers from Other Containers

Spilling over sides of antique wine barrel are ivy geraniums. Planted wine barrel is from Europe, where German gardeners plant flowers in almost anything that will hold soil. Several varieties of plants are usually combined in one container.

Old washtub overflows with brightly colored petunias, single ivy geraniums, and flowering maple. Tub, which sits in front of winery in Europe, was placed on wooden pallet to allow for water drainage through bottom of tub. Tubs could hold small trees instead.

Antique butter churn sits indoors on a wooden stand as a pot holder. One clay pot fits snugly into opening on side of churn. Remove pot for watering.

Planter from the past is this wood and metal umbrella stand.

A Plastic Gutter Window Box

Window sill planter *brings garden indoors, takes up hardly any space. Assorted pinks benefit from generous sunlight. Design: David Hafleigh.*

Containers from Building Materials

Outdoor window box planters are part of every European village, but indoor window boxes are becoming a unique American counterpart.

The boxes can be made from plastic rain gutters, which are durable, easy to work with, need no painting, and are watertight. They can be cut and joined with a few simple tools.

Because the plastic is flexible, the window box works best when layered with gravel and filled with small, individual plastic or clay pots. With some windows, boxes can be mounted on redwood boards and attached at various heights above the sill.

Materials and tools

10 feet of vinyl plastic gutter
2 plastic gutter end caps (right and left)
Fine-toothed handsaw
Sandpaper or wood rasp
Ruler/pencil/exacto knife
PVC primer and cement/brush

How to make

1. Measure the width of the window, allowing clearance for the window opening mechanism.

2. Pencil mark the gutter at a point ¼ inch less than the window measurement. With a handsaw, cut the gutter squarely and sand the ends with sandpaper or a rasp (fig. 1).

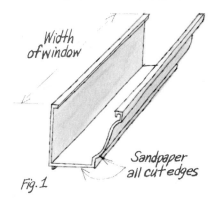

Width of window

Sandpaper all cut edges

Fig. 1

3. Use the knife to cut back the rib on the bottom of the gutter ⅝ inch (fig. 2).

Fig. 2

4. Prime the end caps and gutter end surfaces with PVC surface primer.

5. Apply liberal amount of PVC cement to the inside grooves of end caps and place them in position at the ends of the gutter (fig. 3). Let dry completely before placing plants inside.

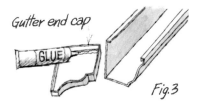

Gutter end cap

GLUE

Fig. 3

Rough, round sewer pipes, *rectangular building blocks, and smooth flue liners of various shapes are some of the best outdoor plant containers available. All of these building materials can be purchased at building supply stores at low prices. The least expensive are the concrete building blocks, sewer pipes, and drainage pipes.*

Blocks, tiles, and liners are ready to plant within seconds—simply place them directly on the ground, fill them with soil, and plant. Redwood chips surround the plant containers pictured on page 62.

Descriptions of the pictured building materials follow:

1. *Flue liner, 21 inches square*
2. *Four-inch-diameter regular sewer pipe, 2 feet high*
3. *Stacked gray standard building blocks, each 8 by 8 by 16 inches*
4. *Four-inch-diameter ABS plastic pipe*
5. *Oval flue liner, 8½ by 17 inches*
6. *Six-inch-diameter terra cotta drain tile*
7. *Round flue liner, 13 inches in diameter*
8. *Double hub regular sewer pipe, 4 inches in diameter*
9. *Six-inch-diameter terra cotta drain tile*
10. *Standard concrete building block, an 8-inch cube, with sash*
11. *Four-inch-diameter steel pipe*
12. *Concrete column block, 12 by 8 by 12 inches*
13. *Gray standard building block, 12 by 8 by 16 inches.*

Versatile Flue Tile

The pristine shape of flue tiles makes a rugged outdoor planter and a creative landscaping element. The clay tiles come in various sizes and in cylindrical or square shapes. Some of these shapes lend themselves to interlocking modular arrangements; others work together in progressive height arrangements.

Being bottomless, the flue tile is converted into a planter in any one of three ways.

The simplest way to use a flue tile as a planter is to sink a tile into the soil an inch or so, fill the tile with soil, and plant.

Another method is to attach chicken wire to the bottom. First drill a hole on either side near the bottom with a masonry drill. Insert two bolts and attach the chicken wire. Line the chicken wire with sphagnum moss (fig. 1). Add soil mix and plant.

For the third method you'll need a sheet of 6-ounce fiberglass-reinforced plastic. Cut the plastic with a fine-tooth saw to fit the bottom of a flue tile. Attach the plastic to the bot-

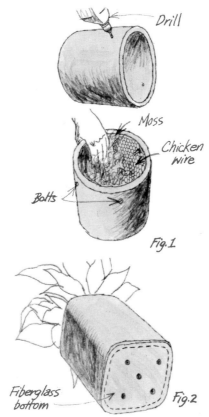

Drill

Moss

Chicken wire

Bolts

Fig. 1

Fiberglass bottom

Fig. 2

tom with epoxy glue. Drill holes in the plastic for drainage and set plants in a loose soil mix (fig. 2).

Place potted mums *in flue tiles to brighten a patio with splash of color.*

Two Planters from One Barrel

Shallow end *of a barrel is 9 inches deep and holds sufficient soil for blue and yellow pansies. Design: Carlton C. Kovell.*

Deep end *of a barrel is planted with Japanese maple. This container is 23½ inches high and 35 inches in diameter.*

Sunken flue tiles *make outdoor containers for bird of paradise. Design: Owen H. Peters.*

Skylit or spotlit, *indoor garden has plants displayed in rugged flue tiles of various sizes. Garden is seen from entry, dining, and living rooms. Design: Robert Chittock.*

Husky barrels, *stained to match house trim, create portable entry garden. Wood pallet holds planters above graveled strip. Design: Talley & Associates.*

Huge barrels—50 to 80-gallon size—make the easiest and strongest wooden plant tubs. A barrel factory should have barrels with staves you can purchase. Cut the barrel in two and drill drainage holes in each bottom.

Though making plant tubs from barrels is nothing new, a unique approach to this planter idea is to cut the barrel so that each part can be used for particular plant types. Cut an 80-gallon barrel, for example, into one large section and one small section. The large one (23 1/2 inches high and 35 inches in diameter) will suit small trees for up to 5 years. To insure your tree's success, drill drainage holes in the barrel's bottom; water and fertilize regularly.

The smaller section of the barrel (about 9 inches deep) can support annual flowers or small shrubs.

Linseed oil on the tub's interior will help stave off wood deterioration. Wood stain applied to the exterior will blend the tub with its environment.

Glass Jugs and a Gallon of Greenery

Gallon-size glass jugs capture miniature gardens within their lucent walls. When a jug is cut in half, both ends become planters: the bottom resembles a bowl; the top is a hanging container when suspended upside down by a macramé sling and plugged at its mouth. The transparent glass—whether green, clear, brown, or orange—reveals carefully layered soil, charcoal, sand, and gravel.

The materials needed to make this container are simple to obtain. For a start, save gallon jugs from wine, vinegar, or fruit juice.

Materials and tools

1-gallon glass jug
Bottle cutter
Kerosene or sewing machine oil
1 yard of heavy yarn or soft twine
Scissors/serrated knife
White glue

(Continued in next column)

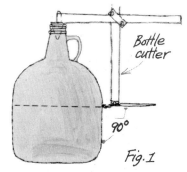

Fig. 1

Quarter-inch "U"-shape leading (quantity depends on jug circumference)
Ruler/pencil

How to make

1. Use a bottle cutter to cut the jug in half; carefully follow the instructions that come with the cutter. Be sure to oil the cutter wheel first with oil or kerosene. Insert the cutter at the desired height and make a clean line on the glass. The glass should make a tearing sound if cut properly. Slowly and lightly tap along the cut line with the metal tapper until fracture line is complete (fig. 1). Twist the top of the jug, holding the bottom firmly in one hand, until the glass separates.

2. Measure the circumference of the cut edge. With a serrated knife, cut a length of leading to fit the cir-

cumference. Separate the edges of the leading with a pencil (fig. 2).

Lead

Fig. 2

3. Form the leading around the top edge of the cut bottle; then lift off the leading and fill the "U" cavity with

Contemporary Coffee Can

Redwood and cotton rope cinched together by an adjustable turnbuckle encase the oft-recycled coffee can.

This plant container is designed with flexibility from all angles. You can cut the can at any point for varied heights. And in place of coffee cans, substitute paint cans, metal pipes, clay pipes, or galvanized heat pipes. You might attach the can modules in a line, creating a long row planter.

The coffee can planter is for use as a decorative sleeve or for cut flowers. If you want to plant directly inside, drill several holes in the bottom of the can and set over a saucer.

Materials and tools

2-pound coffee can
Kiln-dried redwood as follows:
   3 feet of 1 by 4
   2 feet of 1 by 2
   2 feet of 1 by 1
8 feet of 3/32-inch braided
   cotton rope
1 turnbuckle
Twenty 3-penny, 1¼-inch galvanized nails
Polyurethane spray paint

(Continued in next column)

Compass
Saber saw, handsaw, or table saw
Drill/¼-inch, 3/16-inch, and
   hole cutter bits
Hammer/ruler/pencil

How to make

1. With a table saw or handsaw, cut four 8-inch lengths of wood from the 1 by 4.

2. Arrange the 8-inch pieces of wood in groups of 2, each pair forming a rectangle. One pair will be the top, the other the bottom of the planter (fig. 1).

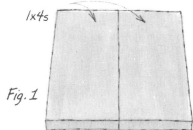

1x4s

Fig. 1

3. For the top of the planter, center the coffee can on the rectangle and draw a pencil line around its circumference. With a compass, draw an-

other circle ¼ inch inside the first; this is the circle you will cut. Each piece of the rectangle should have a half-circle drawn on it.

4. Using a saber saw, cut out the half-circle on each piece.

5. With a handsaw, cut the 1 by 1 and the 1 by 2 into equal lengths to fit across each side of the top and bottom rectangles (fig. 2). The 1 by 1s will be used on the top, the 1 by 2s on the bottom.

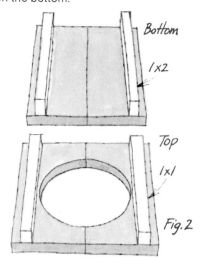

Bottom
1x2
Top
1x1
Fig. 2

white glue. Place a length of yarn or twine in the cavity and trim it to fit (fig. 3).

4. Place the leading, lined with glue and yarn, on the top edge of the bottle and smooth with your fingers. Turn the bottle on its side and then upside down while pressing the leading to the glass with the edge of a pencil (fig. 4).

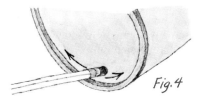

5. Let the glue dry completely before planting.

Carefully layered soil *is revealed through cut gallon jug. Design: Pat Lyman.*

6. Locate the rope holes on either side of the 1 by 2s and the 1 by 1s. Remove the strips and drill with a 3/16-inch bit (fig. 3).

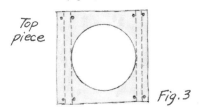

7. Nail the strips to the 1 by 4s from the top and bottom.

8. If drainage is desired, drill a hole in the bottom, using a hole cutter bit.

9. Coat the coffee can with the spray paint. Let dry completely.

10. Assemble the finished pieces with the coffee can in place. Thread the top with the turnbuckle fully extended (fig. 4). Tighten the turnbuckle and the rope will become taut.

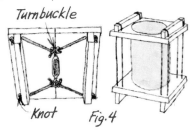

Rope and redwood *support for coffee can creates rustic container for plants or cut flowers. Sweet broom blooms in this planter. Design: Terry Spilsted.*

Copper Sculpture Planter

Green-incrusted copper tubing catches the light on its rose pink sides, creating a vibrant contrast between textures and color. This copper planter is a sculpture whose loose, flowing design interacts with the plant it holds.

You needn't be a skilled metal worker to make this design, but you do need to take extreme care when handling the flame and acids. Work carefully and slowly. The finished planter is worth the effort—it is unique and will last a lifetime.

Materials and tools

New or used copper tubing of varied diameters (amount depends on planter size and tube diameters)
1 sheet of 20-ounce copper (sheet size determined by planter size)
Leather gloves/rubber gloves
⅛-inch solder
Long-nose pliers
Tin snips
Hacksaw
Wire brush
Soldering acid/brush
Fine emery paper
Propane torch
Vice grips
Copper wire or disassembled coat hanger
Pencil/paper
Measuring tape
Clear plastic spray paint

How to make

1. Select various lengths of copper tubing in ½ to ¾-inch diameters (inside dimensions).

2. To determine the amount of pipe to be used, measure the circumference of the pot you will use. (If you are going to plant directly in the planter you won't need this measurement.) You can plan any size or shape, using pipe as needed.

3. Lay out the copper pipe in a variety of lengths, the bottom edges forming a straight line (fig. 1).

4. Trim the pipe to desired lengths, making all cuts square for easier soldering. The length of pipes as laid

Freeform container *of soldered copper pipes has green patina added for unusual color and texture. (Color photo is on page 3.) Design: Hal Pastorius.*

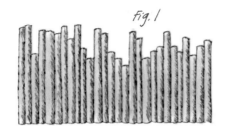

Fig. 1

out should be slightly less than the desired circumference.

5. If you're using a pot inside the planter, place the pot upside-down on the paper and draw a line around its circumference. Add to this the outside dimension of your largest pipe. This is the pattern for cutting your copper base (fig. 2). Make a paper pattern from this and place it on a sheet of copper. Cut the circle out with the tin snips. Do not attempt to follow the outline closely—some overhang will give the planter character and make it easier to solder later. If you are not using a round pot, sketch an outline on paper that you want to have as the bottom.

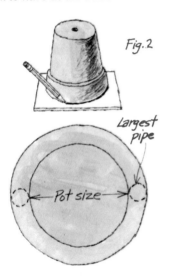

Fig. 2

Largest pipe

Pot size

6. Clean all copper before soldering. To do this, dip the pipe in commercial soldering acid or dilute nitric acid. *Caution:* Acid is caustic poison; use rubber gloves and protective clothing. A safer but slower way to clean copper is to sand it with fine emery or sandpaper (fig. 3).

Fig. 3

7. Tin all the surfaces to be soldered. Brush all the surfaces with soldering acid. Carefully run the torch flame near the surface, close enough so that it will transfer the heat to melt the solder. Cover the surfaces with a bright coating of solder at the points of contact (the outside edge of the copper bottom and the bottom ends of all copper pipes). Tin also 2 points of contact on each pipe to be joined. You can use the acid brush to smear the solder around (fig. 4).

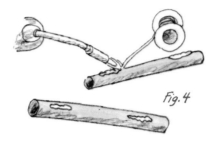

Fig. 4

8. Solder all the pipes together in pairs. If drainage is desired, leave unsoldered spaces near the bottom. While soldering the pairs together, hold the pipes with the long-nose pliers and wear leather gloves.

9. Solder the paired pipes to the bottom, following your outline (fig. 5).

Fig. 5

You can solder pipes with a clay pot in place if you don't touch the pot with the flame.

10. Wrap wire around all the pipes and solder all unsoldered pipes to each other at 2 points (fig. 6).

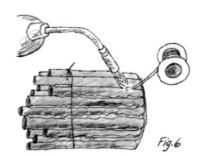

Fig. 6

11. Add extra solder around the bottom for reinforcement. Remove the wire.

12. If you want to add a patina to the copper you can experiment with different formulas for different colors. Try garden fertilizers, ammonia glass cleaners, bleach, and other mild corrosives. (Do not mix ammonia and bleach.) To add a patina, strip off all oxides by sanding or using acid. Spray or paint the solution on the planter while it is still warm from soldering. After patina has developed, remove any residual solution by running water over it. Some patinas take minutes to develop; others take days. A clear plastic spray paint will protect the patina and bring out the colors.

Three variations for a copper planter

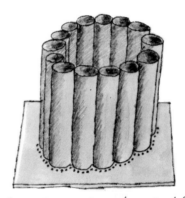

Pipes of same size cut evenly at tops

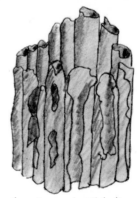

Irregular pipes cut with heliarc torch

Bent and irregular pipes

Containers from the Unexpected

Fabric with a Flare

Using fabric to make a plant container opens a spectrum of possibilities for color, texture, pattern, and shape. You can model fabric to form loose, freeform shapes or, by quilting or lining the fabric, you can make it resemble rigid forms. Choose a fabric to blend with the design of a room or a fabric that could play a part in the design of the planter itself. Vinyl-coated cloth is practical because it is water-resistant and easy to clean.

Materials and tools

8-inch clay pot with nonporous saucer
¼ yard of 36-inch or 45-inch-wide fabric (quilted, patterned, plain, or vinyl)
½ yard of 36-inch or 45-inch-wide fabric in a contrasting pattern or color for lip, bottom, and lining
Sewing machine
Scissors/thread/pins
Cotton or dacron batting or nylon stockings (if you're doing your own quilting)
Paper/pencil
Measuring tape

How to make

1. Quilt fabric (if you're doing it yourself) before you cut out the pattern pieces.

2. Cut a paper pattern and then cut out the fabric (fig. 1).

Quilted sleeve *carries country motif. Design: Lynne Morrall.*

If you enjoy working with your hands, you probably have a craft skill you can use to make a plant container. Perhaps you know how to sew—then try making a fabric sleeve for a pot. If you crochet, work up a textured disguise for a clay pot. Or if the art of stained glass is your forte, consider a stained-glass terrarium. This chapter gives these and other skills a workout.

Almost any craft skill can be tapped to make a plant container. Craft projects range from decorating the exterior of a store bought clay pot (see pages 40-45) to making an original container of your own design.

Some materials used in crafts should be modified for use with plants and moisture. A waterproof coating and a reinforced, sturdy form are essential—a resin finish or clear plastic spray comes in handy for both.

Here are some craft skills you may never have thought of applying to plant containers:
- Silk screening patterns on paper, then gluing the paper to the outside of a clay pot
- Enameling the exterior of a copper container
- Appliquéing a fabric planter sleeve
- Knitting a planter sleeve from yarn
- Woodcarving designs on a basic wooden box planter
- Vegetable stamping decoration on clay pots
- Wire sculpturing a bowl-like shape to be filled with sphagnum moss and planted
- Sandpainting designs on clay pots
- Quilting pot sleeves
- Beading pot sleeves
- Cutting paper to decorate clay pots

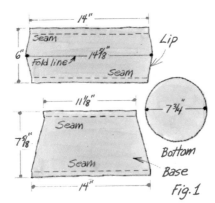

Fig. 1

3. With right sides together, sew the base pieces together along 1 side seamline; repeat with base lining pieces. Press seams open (fig. 2).

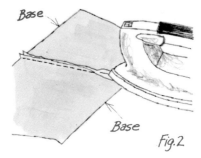

Fig. 2

4. Sew lip pieces together along 1 side seamline. Clip at the point and press seam open (fig. 3).

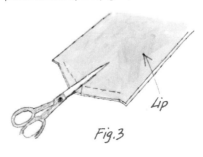

Fig. 3

5. Sew the lip to top edge of base. Sew the other long edge of the lip to edge of base lining. Press seams toward lip (fig. 4).

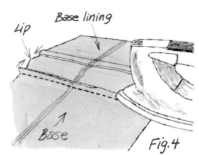

Fig. 4

6. With right sides together, fold fabric in half along side seam. Sew the other side in one continuous motion—base, lip, and lining all at once (fig. 5).

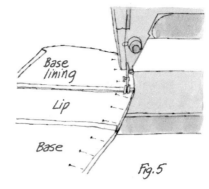

Fig. 5

7. Turn the fabric right side out and fold the lip in half along the fold line. Fill the lip with stuffing material if you want the lip to appear full.

8. Pin through all layers at the seam line that joins the lip to the base, keeping the seams on top of each other. Top stitch through all layers on the seam line (fig. 6).

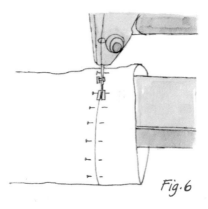

Fig. 6

9. Pin the bottom edges of the base together. Gather the bottom outside and the bottom lining slightly along the seam line. Pin the outside bottom to the lower edge of the base, easing the fabric in where necessary (fig. 7).

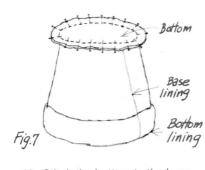

Fig. 7

10. Stitch the bottom to the base. Press the seam allowance in toward the center of the base.

11. Fold in the seam allowance along the seam line on the bottom lining. Pin in place and hand stitch the lining to the seam line of the base and bottom.

12. Place a saucer and pot inside the sleeve. Fold the lip over to form a cuff.

Crocheted Containers

The popularity of macramé planter covers and plant slings almost guarantees the appeal of a knobby, crocheted planter cover, since they resemble each other.

Instructions for two planter covers are on these pages: one is made with cotton macramé twine and is combined with a pot hanger; the other is a natural jute planter cover. Both are inexpensive to make and require a basic knowledge of crochet skills.

Here are the stitches needed for these planter covers:

CHAIN STITCH

Insert hook into slip knot; wrap yarn around hook clockwise

Pull yarn through loop on hook

SINGLE CROCHET

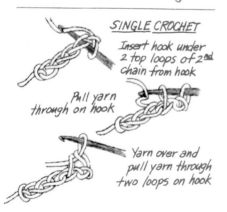

Insert hook under 2 top loops of 2nd chain from hook

Pull yarn through on hook

Yarn over and pull yarn through two loops on hook

DOUBLE CROCHET

Chain stitch

Yarn over hook and insert hook into 4th chain from hook; yarn over and pull through loop

Yarn over and pull through 2 loops on hook; yarn over and pull through remaining 2 loops

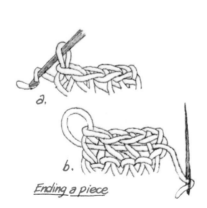

a,

b,

Ending a piece

Materials and tools

Granny Square Planter Cover:

1 ball (about 250 yards) of 3-ply cotton macramé twine, size 24
J aluminum crochet hook or hook to give proper gauge
Scissors
(Gauge: one complete square measures 5½ by 5½ inches)

Natural Jute Planter Cover:

100 yards of 3-ply jute or rug yarn
K aluminum crochet hook or hook to give proper gauge
Scissors
(Gauge: 3 stitches=1 inch; 1 row=1 inch)

Granny squares *of crocheted cotton macramé twine combine to make a container sleeve. Design: Jane Hummert.*

How to make

Granny Square Planter Cover (for one 6-inch plant pot):

Make 5 granny squares:
1. Ch 6, join with sl st to form ring. *Row 1:* Ch 3, 2 dc in ring, ch 3, *3 dc in ring, ch 3, repeat from * twice. Join with sl st to top of 1st ch-3.
Row 2: Ch 3, turn, 2 dc in ch-3 space of previous row (not 1st ch-3). Ch 3, 3 dc in same ch-3 space, ch 1 (this forms the corner). *3 dc, ch 3, 3 dc, ch 1 in next ch-3 space. Repeat from * in the next 2 spaces. Join with sl st to top of 1st ch-3 of row 2.
Row 3: Ch 3, 2 dc, ch 1 in middle space. *3 dc, ch 3, 3 dc, ch 1 in corner, 3 dc, ch 1 in middle sp. Repeat from * 2 more times, 3 dc, ch 3 3 dc, ch 1 in last corner. To finish, sl st to top of 1st ch-3 or row 3. End off.
2. Using 1 square as a base and the other 4 for sides, sl st squares together on all edges, then sc around the top of the planter. To make the straps, start in one corner of the planter cover and make a ch 30 inches long; attach with sl st to opposite corner. Ch 1, turn, and sl st in each ch across to original corner. Repeat for other strap.

Natural Jute Planter Cover
(7 inches tall by 7 inches in diameter):

1. Beginning at center bottom, ch 4, join to 1st ch with sl st to form a ring.

2. Round 1: Ch 3, 11 dc in ring, join with sl st to top of ch-3 (ch 3 will count as 1st dc).

Round 2: Ch 3, dc in 1st st, 2 dc in each st around (24 sts). Join with sl st.

Round 3: Ch 3, dc in 1st st, 2 dc in each st around (48 sts). Join with sl st. If diameter is not large enough, repeat round 3 until correct size. Number of sts in this round must be a multiple of 3, and this number will be the same in each round from now on. The base of the planter sleeve is now completed.

Round 4: Ch 1. With hook coming from back to front, sc in the back loop of each st around. Join with sl st.

Round 5: Ch 3, dc in each st around (48 sts). Join with sl st.

Round 6: Ch 5, *skip 2 sts, dc in next st, ch 2. Repeat from * around. Join to 3rd ch.

Round 7: Repeat round 5.

Round 8: Repeat round 6.

Rounds 9-10: Repeat round 5. (If cover is not tall enough, repeat rounds 6 and 5 until desired height. End with a round 5.) End off and weave in yarn.

Earthen-tone jute *planter sleeve accents house plants. Design: Tina Kaufmann.*

Stained-glass Terrarium

Transparent, opalescent, and opaque pieces of polychromatic glass are fused together with copper foil and solder to form a birdhouselike terrarium for indoor plants. The glass colors interplay with those of the plants contained in the miniature semienclosed garden.

Because the planter lacks drainage, be sure to use a layer of gravel, charcoal, or vermiculite with the potting soil; water sparingly.

Materials and tools

Cathedral, window, and opalescent glass blanks in the following sizes and quantities:

	Cathedral	Window	Opalescent
A	10½″ x 5¼″	10½″ x 10½″	
B			
C			10½″ x 6½″
C-rev			
D	10½″ x 1¼″		
E	6½″ x 9 3/16″	6½″ x 6 9/16″	
Bottom		9″ x 9″ Dbl. strength	

1 pound of 60/40 or 50/50 solid core ⅛-inch solder
36-yard roll of ¼-inch copper foil
Masking tape
Glass cutter
Paper/pencil/marking pen
Soldering iron or gun, 60-200 watts
Flux
Glass cleaner or glass wax/rag
Scissors
Rubber cement/brush

How to make

1. Cut paper patterns as shown on this page.
2. Place the patterns directly on the glass, using rubber cement to hold them in place. With a glass cutter, make slow, deliberate strokes on the glass along the edge of the patterns. (Each cut requires only one stroke. More than one stroke increases the probability of damaging the cutter or cracking the glass. Practice glass cutting on scrap glass before making these cuts. If you haven't cut glass before, make this planter using glass

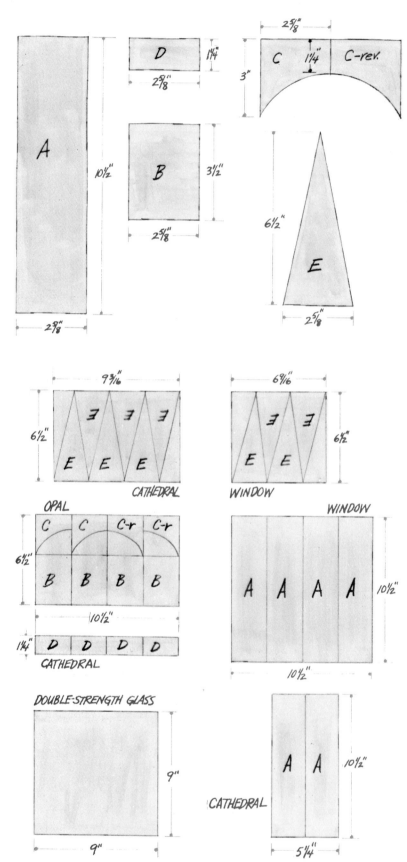

PATTERNS FOR GLASS PLANTER

that is smooth on both sides.) After you have made one stroke on the glass, use a table edge to apply pressure on the glass to break it. Mark each piece with the correct letter, according to the patterns.

3. Wrap copper foil around the edges of each piece of cut glass; use your fingers or a small piece of wood to smooth the edges (fig. 1).

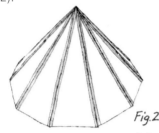

4. Lay out E pieces. Tape them together with masking tape. Turn over the ¾ circle of E pieces. Tape the first and last pieces together, forming a cone with the tape on the inside (fig. 2).

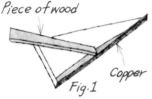

5. Apply flux to the copper foil on the outside of the cone. Solder the seams of the cone on the outside. The cone is sturdy enough to tilt if supported by a jar or block. Remove the tape and solder the inside seams one at a time on a level surface (fig. 3).

6. Lay out the midsection pieces flat, inside up, using a ruler to line up the side and bottom edges. Tape them together and stand the panel upright. Bend it around into a cylinder and tape the first and last pieces together. Solder the pieces together as you did for the cone section. Tape the cone to the mid-section (fig. 4).

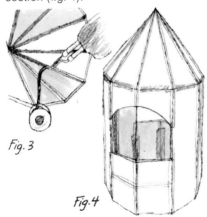

Golden hues of stained glass radiate warmth to house plants arrangement. Panamiga, aluminum plant, and variegated peperomia enjoy humidity. Design: Steven Skaroff.

7. Solder the cone onto the midsection, making sure the seams of the cone and the seams of the midsection form continuous lines.

8. Place planter on a 9-inch square of double-strength (DS) window glass. Write "up" on the top side of DS glass with a marking pen. Put an arrow on any one piece of the midsection and another arrow on the DS glass opposite the first arrow, inside the planter. This enables you to line up the corresponding sides later. With the midsection standing on the DS glass, draw a line along the inside edges (fig. 5).

9. With the glass cutter, cut out the bottom piece. Each angled cut should be made one at a time and broken along a table edge.

10. Foil the bottom piece and smooth the edges. Set the planter

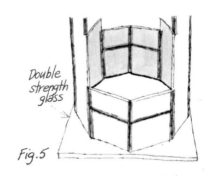

on the bottom and solder the joints.

11. Flux and solder all remaining copper, inside and out.

12. Clean the planter with glass cleaner or glass wax. (To give the metal a copper look, use a solution of 1 teaspoon copper sulfate in 2 gallons of water. Rub the metal with a rag dipped in the solution; then rinse.)

Five Easy Pieces of Tile

Five glazed ceramic tiles fit snugly together to form a square container for a potted plant. Boldly patterned tiles or plain terra cotta tiles are available in tile stores or gift shops.

Even though the inside is water-proofed, be sure to remove the plant for watering. Let the pot drain before putting it back in the container.

Materials and tools

Five ceramic tiles, 4¼ or 6 inches square, 3/16 or ¼ inch thick, lugged or unlugged
2 feet of ¼ inch quarter-round wood molding
Ceramic epoxy

(Continued on next page)

Sunburst design *on ceramic tile container enhances prayer plant. Wood molding and glue hold planter together. Use purchased tiles or handcraft your own.*

A Container Tied in Knots

Macramé—not to be confused with basketry—can be used to make containers that look like Indian coiled baskets. Made with the two basic knots shown below, this flared container works best as a sleeve for a clay or plastic pot.

Depending on the type of plant you plan to display, make the container brilliantly textured or soft and subtle by experimenting with a variety of colors. To protect the string from mold, line the container with foil or plastic.

Materials and tools

1 ball of heavy green cord or sisal twine
1 large ball of green cable cord
½ ball of cable cord in *each* of the following colors: orange, maroon, white
Scissors
White glue
Clay or plastic pot (your shaping guide)

How to make

1. Cut sixteen 4-yard lengths of green cable cord and dip each end into white glue to prevent unraveling.
2. Starting 1 inch from the end of the heavy cord, attach 12 of the 16 lengths of cable cord at their midpoints with reverse mounting knots (fig. 1).

3. Taper the core cord to a point; then bend the cord to form a circle wide enough for the drainage hole of the pot. To join the core into a round, attach the remaining 4 cable cord lengths over *both* the tapered end and the beginning of the second round (fig. 2).

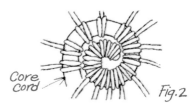

Core Cord

Fig. 2

4. Using the 32 ends from the first round as working cords, begin to knot tight double half hitches over the core. Continue to knot and coil in an outward spiral until 6½ concentric rounds are formed. Cut 4-yard cord lengths as needed and add in, using reverse mounting knots where open spaces occur.
5. To begin the sides of the container, position the core to lie slightly above the previous round and gradually work rounds up and outward from there, continuing to knot double half hitches as you go. Using

BASIC KNOTS TO KNOW

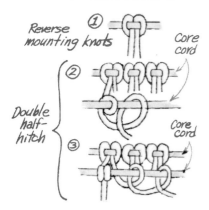

Reverse mounting knots ①
Core cord

Double half-hitch ②
Core cord

③

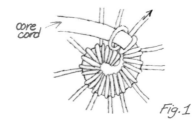

core cord

Fig. 1

Handsaw
Wax paper
Rubber bands
Silicone sealer/brush

How to make

1. With the handsaw, cut 4 pieces of molding the same height as your tiles.

2. Cover your work surface with wax paper so the tiles won't stick to it as you work. Apply a ribbon of ceramic epoxy to the 4 outside edges of the bottom tile and along the facing inside bottom edge of each of the side tiles (fig. 1).

Fig. 1

3. When the adhesive is no longer tacky to the touch, apply a second coating and immediately join the tiles in an upright position (fig. 2).

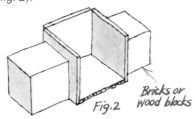

Fig. 2   Bricks or wood blocks

4. Without gluing, place cut lengths of molding at corners and secure with 1 or more rubber bands. You may have to realign the tiles while the adhesive is still pliable (fig. 3).

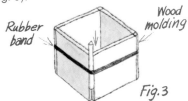

Rubber band   Wood molding   *Fig. 3*

5. When tiles are firmly in place (you needn't wait for adhesive to dry), remove the bands and molding. Apply adhesive to the flat sides of the molding and to the edges of the tiles at the corners. Set molding in place and replace rubber bands (fig. 4).

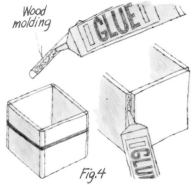

Wood molding   *Fig. 4*

6. When the adhesive is dry, you can make the container sufficiently moistureproof by applying a liberal coat of silicone sealer to the inside with a brush or tube.

---

reverse mounting knots, add in 4-yard cord lengths where open spaces occur. Work these new cords in with more double half hitches.

6. For the color design, attach contrasting cable cord with reverse mounting knots at 4 equidistant points on the next round. Each of the 4 triangular areas shown was started from 2 white and 4 maroon 4-yard lengths of cable cord. As the designs grow wider, more strands are added using the method shown in figure 3. Orange cord is eventually added as an accent to the middle of each design area in the 14th round.

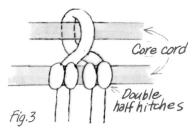

Core cord   Double half hitches   *Fig. 3*

7. Shape the basket by curving the core sharply outward at points midway between each design area.

8. When 26 rounds have been knotted, cut off the core near one corner of the container and taper this cut end. Knot firmly over the taper.

9. Cut all ends to 1 inch; then glue them to the inside of the basket lip.

Tidy knots tied *around a main core form patterned sides of decorative sleeve for indoor plants. (Color photo is on page 3.) Design: Nilda Duffek.*

Laced Leather Sleeve

A simple leather sleeve can camouflage a clay or plastic container of any size. Made from one piece of leather, the sleeve has four corners that are laced, gently flaring the sides outward. To prevent the sleeve from getting moldy from pot moisture, spray the inside with silicone, coat with a wax, or line with foil or plastic. Place a nonporous clay or plastic saucer in the bottom of the sleeve before inserting the pot.

Materials and tools

2 square feet of 8 or 9-ounce leather
Leather dye/rag (optional)
Heavy waxed nylon thread
#3 edge beveler
3/32-inch thonging chisel, small hole punch, or nail

(Continued on next page)

Bold, rugged feeling *of leather sleeve offsets delicate leaves of jacaranda seedling. Roomy container holds clay pot with saucer. Design: Christine Mattson.*

Understanding Those Technical Terms

Variety, imagination, whimsy *show in plant containers on filigree-edged window ledge in Spain. Ceramic pots, eggshells, tin cans are among items giving spontaneous effect.*

Bevel. To make a cut through wood at an angle other than 90° (fig. 1).

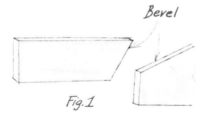

Bevel

Fig. 1

Blind dado. A dado that occurs between the edges but not through the edges of a piece of wood (fig. 2).

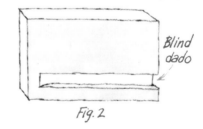

Blind dado

Fig. 2

Butt joint. A joint made by fastening two squarely cut pieces of wood together without fitting one into the other. Butt joints are weak and must be reinforced (fig. 3).

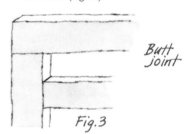

Butt joint

Fig. 3

Caulk. To plug or fill seams or crevices with a sealant.

Dado. To cut a notch whose depth is half the thickness of the wood that is to be inserted into the notch (fig. 4).

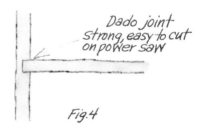

Dado joint strong, easy to cut on power saw

Fig. 4

. . . Materials and tools (cont'd.)

Razor knife
Tape measure
1 sheet of cardboard or heavy paper
Pencil or waterproof felt marker
Scissors

How to make

1. With a tape measure, measure the pot's height and its top and bottom diameters.

2. Make a pattern of heavy paper or cardboard, using the pencil or marker and all 3 measurements (fig. 1).

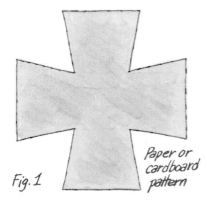

Fig. 1

Paper or cardboard pattern

3. Trace the pattern on the leather, using the marker. Cut out the shape with a razor knife.

4. Bevel the top edges of the container.

5. Dye the leather if you want a darker color. Follow the directions on the bottle and apply evenly with the rag.

6. Use a black leather dye or the felt marker to blacken all beveled and cut edges.

7. Punch sewing holes with the thonging chisel ⅛ inch from the edges to be seamed (fig. 2). You can use a small hole punch or a small nail.

Fig. 2

8. Use the nylon thread for sewing the seams. Starting from the inside bottom, proceed all the way up the sides with diagonal stitches, skipping every other hole. Go back down through the skipped holes to complete the cross stitches (fig. 3).

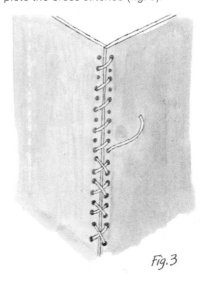

Fig. 3

9. Coat the inside of the leather sleeve with a protective seal or line with waterproof material.

Fence. A guard attached to a table saw or radial-arm saw for controlling the location and extent of a cut.

Flux. A substance that promotes the fusing of metals; purifies and prevents undue oxidation of metal surfaces.

Grog. Finely ground, fired clay added to clay body to reduce shrinkage and plasticity or to impart texture.

Half-lap joint. A joining of two pieces of wood made by cutting away half the thickness of each piece so that the pieces fit together with surfaces flush (fig. 5).

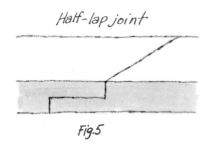

Half-lap joint

Fig. 5

Kerf. The narrow cut made by a saw, the thickness of the saw blade; the

process of cutting small grooves across a board (fig. 6).

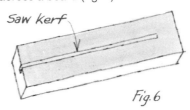

Saw kerf

Fig. 6

Lath. A thin strip of wood usually measuring about 1½ inches wide, ⅜ inch thick, 4 feet long.

Miter. To join in an angular shape two pieces of wood beveled at equal angles (fig. 7).

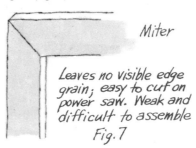

Miter

Leaves no visible edge grain; easy to cut on power saw. Weak and difficult to assemble

Fig. 7

Miter box. A device whose sides are slotted to guide a handsaw in the

making of accurate angular cuts for a mitered joint (fig. 8).

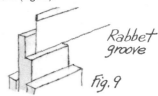

Miter box

Fig. 8

Rabbet. To cut a groove at the end or along the edge of a piece of wood to receive another piece of wood similarly cut. The two cuts meet each other at right angles at the end of the board (fig. 9).

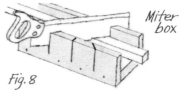

Rabbet groove

Fig. 9

Rip. To saw or split wood lengthwise of the grain or fiber.

Stop. A device used on a table saw or radial-arm saw to limit the size of cuts; used to make repeated cuts of the same width or length.

Tin. To coat or cover with tin.

Index

Photographers

William Aplin: 16 (right), 65 (top right). **Kathy Brenzel:** 61 (top left, right). **Glenn Christiansen:** 29 (top), 43 (top), 56. **Richard Dawson:** 13 (top, bottom left). **Gerald R. Fredrick:** 12, 52, 53. **Jack McDowell:** 3 (left), 27 (top), 33 (top), 54 (bottom right), 60 (bottom left, right), 61 (bottom left, right), 75. **Ells Marugg:** 3 (center, right), 6, 11, 14, 16 (left), 17 (top right, bottom right), 19, 21, 22, 24, 27 (bottom), 30, 33 (bottom), 35, 38, 40-41, 43 (bottom), 46, 48, 51, 54 (left, top right), 59, 62, 64 (top), 67, 68, 70, 72, 73, 77, 78 (top). **Don Normark:** 9 (bottom right), 13 (bottom right), 64 (bottom left, right), 65 (top left, bottom). **Richard B. Morrall:** 78 (bottom). **Norman A. Plate:** 17 (top center, bottom left, center), 60 (top left). **Martha Rosman:** 57 (top left). **Don Ryan:** 36. **Darrow M. Watt:** 20, 37 (top), 44, 45, 57 (top right, bottom), 60 (top right), 76. **Peter Whiteley:** 17 (top left).